DUMPLINGS

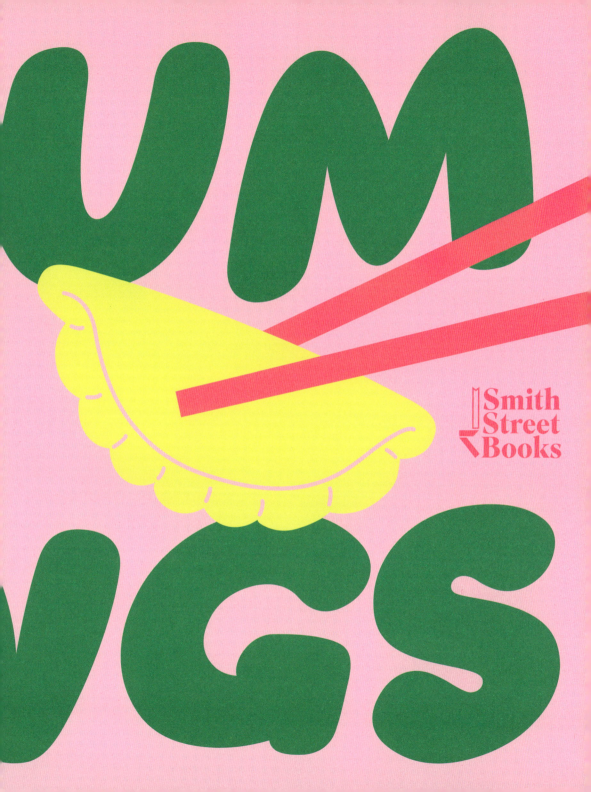

10 STEAMED

54 FRIED

88 BOILED

136 SWEET

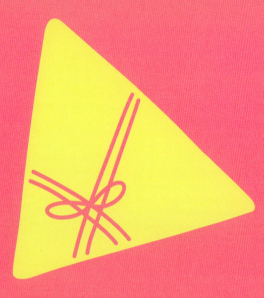

160 BASICS

Introduction	6
Dumpling essentials	8
Folding techniques	174
Index	180

INTRODUCTION

Everybody loves dumplings – that's just a fact. Small in size yet big on flavour, these delightful parcels are a staple all over the world. But who deserves credit for this genius invention? History points to Zhang Zhongjing, a Chinese physician who first made dumplings to remedy frostbitten ears during the Eastern Han dynasty. Fittingly, they're called jiaozi, meaning 'tender ears' in Mandarin.

Whether eaten in the morning at dim sum or as a late-night snack, these plump pockets have evolved from a frostbite cure to a staple in Asian cuisine. Their cultural importance runs as deep as their flavour, with many dumplings shaped like gold ingots (ancient Chinese currency), symbolising wealth and prosperity, which is why many Asian families eat dumplings on New Year's Eve.

The opening of the Silk Road for trade between Asia and Europe gave birth to many global variations, like Japanese gyoza, Korean mandu, and even Italian ravioli and Polish pierogi further afield. Whether sweet or savoury, steamed, boiled or fried – each dumpling delivers the comforting warmth of a hug from within.

This book contains a diverse collection of recipes from all around Asia, including China, Vietnam, Nepal, Korea, Thailand and Japan.

Just like a dim sum trolley, the Steamed section is loaded with classics, including juicy Siu mai (page 12) and Pork xiao long bao (page 18). If you like your dumplings crispy and golden, turn to the Fried section for Prawn wontons (page 56), Thung thong (page 66) or Traditional Japanese pork gyozas (page 72). There are plenty of options for vegetarians across the book, including in the Boiled chapter, with Vegan mushroom & cabbage dumplings (page 92) packed full of umami flavour and Spicy pumpkin & tofu dumplings (page 95) providing subtle sweetness. Got a sweet tooth? Check out the Sweet section for Sago zongzi (page 146) and Hanami dango (page 152).

The Basics chapter has five different dumpling wrapper recipes that can be used across the recipes in this book – though store-bought ones work perfectly if you're short on time (we won't tell anyone!). That said, making them from scratch is worth the extra effort. There are also some handy tips for folding a few classic dumpling shapes at the end of the book, but if you get stuck, there are plenty of videos online that can help you fold, seal and pinch your dumplings perfectly. But no matter how you fold them, the dumplings in this book are sure to be delicious!

DUMPLING ESSENTIALS

When in doubt, just head to your local Asian supermarket for these ingredients.

BAMBOO LEAVES
Bamboo leaves are commonly used to wrap and steam dumplings like Hokkien bak chang (page 116). The leaves add a subtly sweet flavour and aroma to whatever has been wrapped inside. Dried bamboo leaves are available at Asian supermarkets. They need to be cleaned and soaked before using (see page 178 for instructions).

CHINKIANG BLACK VINEGAR
A fermented rice vinegar also known as 'Zhenjiang', which is commonly used in Chinese cooking. Black in colour, it is moderately sour and slightly sweet, with a malty and slightly smoky flavour.

DRIED SHRIMP
Common across Asian cuisines, sun-dried shrimp are popular for their unique taste that packs a sweet umami flavour. Shrunk to the size of a thumbnail, their flavour is a whole lot larger.

GLUTINOUS RICE FLOUR
Glutinous rice flour, derived from glutinous rice (or sticky rice), is essential for creating the chewy textures in dishes like Banh it tran (page 48), Tang yuan (page 138 & 142) and Hanami dango (page 152). Meanwhile, rice flour, ground from regular rice, is primarily used to thicken sauces and soups. They should not be used interchangeably.

GOCHUGARU
These Korean chilli flakes (also called Korean chilli powder), are widely used in Korean dishes. Gochugaru usually comes in two forms: coarse chilli flakes or fine powder.

JICAMA
Jicama or yam bean can usually be found at an Asian supermarket. Alternatively, you can substitute it with water chestnuts or turnip.

DUMPLINGS

MIRIN
A rice wine common in Japanese cooking, with an alcohol content lower than sake's. Mirin brings a sweeter note to dishes with a subtle hit of tang.

PANDAN LEAVES
Popular across Southeast Asia, this aromatic ingredient is added to both sweet and savoury dishes. Commonly compared to vanilla, though with grassier notes, pandan leaves are sold fresh, frozen and dried.

POTATO STARCH
Extracted from potatoes, this neutral-tasting starch is primarily used as a thickening agent for soups and sauces. It's also an excellent binder for Crystal dumpling wrappers (page 162), improving the dough's elasticity and making it easier to roll and shape without breaking.

PRAWN MEAT
This refers to the clean peeled flesh weight of a prawn (shrimp) after the head, tail, shell and intestinal vein have been removed. While it is possible to buy uncooked prawn meat, it is always better to buy fresh prawns and peel and devein them yourself for the recipes in this book.

SHAOXING RICE WINE
This rice wine is key to Chinese cooking and is used in dishes ranging from soups to wontons. It adds a complexity to dishes, introducing a rich, nutty flavour that creates a depth in anything you add it to.

WHEAT STARCH
A popular thickening agent in Asian cuisines, wheat starch is derived by separating the starch from the wheat's protein, fibre and other components. It helps create a smooth, elastic dough for Crystal dumpling wrappers (page 162), which become chewy and translucent once steamed.

DUMPLING ESSENTIALS

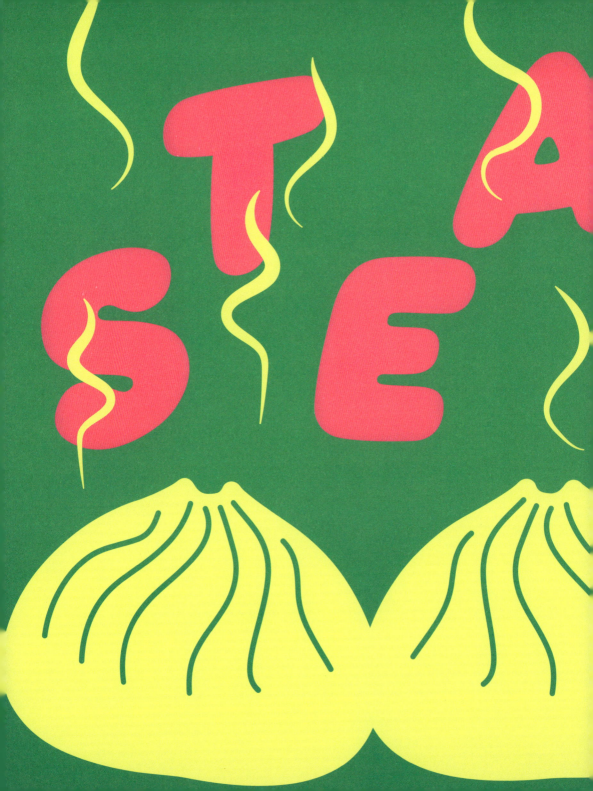

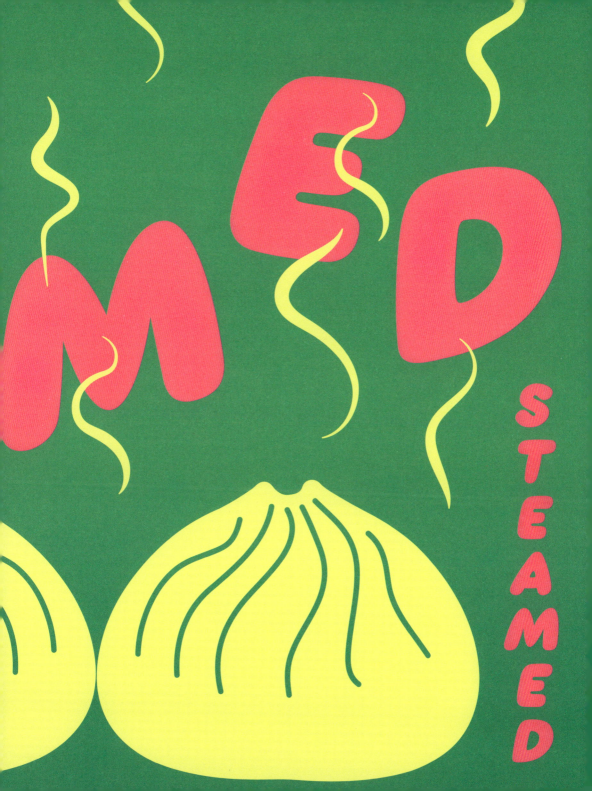

SIU MAI

Originally a star of dim sum cuisine in Guangdong province, siu mai (or shumai) now fly off dim sum trolleys around the world. The open-topped dumplings are packed with a juicy blend of minced pork and fresh prawns, all tucked into a delicate wonton wrapper and steamed to perfection.

MAKES 15

15 Wonton wrappers (page 163), trimmed with a round cookie cutter

½ carrot, finely diced, to garnish

Soy, vinegar and ginger dipping sauce (page 165), to serve

FILLING

3 large dried shiitake mushrooms

200 g (7 oz) minced (ground) pork, 30% fat

100 g (3½ oz) raw prawn (shrimp) meat, roughly chopped

1 tsp vegetable oil

1 tbsp sesame oil

MARINADE

1 tbsp oyster sauce

2 tsp light soy sauce

¼ tsp salt

1 tsp white sugar

2 tsp cornflour (corn starch)

½ tsp baking soda

2 tbsp mushroom soaking water (reserved from above)

½ tsp ground white pepper

To make the filling, soak the shiitake mushrooms in hot water for at least 2 hours to rehydrate them. Drain, reserving 2 tablespoons of the mushroom soaking water for the marinade. Squeeze all the excess water from the mushrooms, then finely chop.

Place the pork in a large bowl with the marinade ingredients. Using chopsticks or your hands, stir the mixture vigorously into a sticky paste, which will take 2–3 minutes.

Add the chopped shiitake mushrooms, prawns, and the vegetable and sesame oils, then stir gently for another minute until well combined. Cover and marinate in the fridge overnight.

To make the dumplings, form an 'O' shape with your thumb touching your index and third finger and lay a wonton wrapper on top. Using a small cake spatula or the back of a spoon, scoop a heaped teaspoon of filling in the centre of the wrapper, then gently push the wrapper and filling into the hole between your fingers while holding the 'O' shape, continue filling the dumpling while holding this shape until the whole wrapper is filled. Add more filling if it is not enough. Garnish the dumpling with the finely diced carrot. Repeat with the remaining filling and wrappers.

Line a large bamboo steamer basket with a round sheet of baking paper with a few holes punched in it (see note). Working in batches, place the dumplings in the steamer, being sure not to overcrowd the basket. Cover and steam over a wok of hot simmering water over medium–high heat for 8–10 minutes, until cooked. Serve immediately.

NOTE: To line a bamboo steamer basket with baking paper, cut out a round sheet of baking paper to fit the bottom of the basket. Fold it into quarters, then punch a few holes in the paper using a hole punch. Unfold the paper and spread it out in the steamer basket before placing the dumplings on top.

HAR GOW

Traditionally served in bamboo baskets at dim sum houses, har gow is the jewel in the crown of the dumpling world. Wrapped in a delicate, translucent skin made from wheat and potato starch, they're filled with fresh prawns and a touch of pork fat for added richness. The result? A plump, pillowy parcel of pure joy.

MAKES 15

15 Crystal dumpling wrappers (page 162)

Crispy garlic chilli oil (page 165), to serve (optional)

FILLING

150 g (5½ oz) raw prawn (shrimp) meat, cut into small pieces

½ tsp salt

½ tsp ground white pepper

30 g (1 oz) bamboo shoots, finely diced

20 g (¾ oz) pork fat, finely diced

1 tsp pork lard

1 tsp sesame oil

1 tsp white sugar

1 tsp cornflour (corn starch)

To make the filling, place the prawn meat in a bowl and sprinkle with the salt and white pepper. Massage together using your hands for about 5 minutes, until slimy. Add the remaining ingredients and stir with your hand until well mixed. Cover and marinate in the fridge for 1 hour.

Using the gyoza folding technique on page 177, fold your wrappers around the filling.

Line a large bamboo steamer basket with a round sheet of baking paper with a few holes punched in it (see note, page 12). Working in batches, place the dumplings in the steamer, being sure not to overcrowd the basket. Cover and steam over a wok of hot simmering water over medium–high heat for 8–10 minutes, until cooked. Serve immediately, with chilli oil if desired.

XO Scallop & Prawn Dumplings

These plump, flavourful dumplings are made with the same crystal dumpling wrapper that surround Har gow dumplings (page 14), but this time they envelop a decadent filling of scallops and prawns. They are then topped with a spoonful of XO sauce – a popular condiment from Hong Kong that is sometimes referred to as 'caviar of the East'. Recipes for XO sauce can vary but it tends to contain dried prawns, dried scallops, ham, garlic, onions and chillis.

MAKES 15

15 Crystal dumpling wrappers (page 162)

XO sauce, to serve

fried shallots, to serve

FILLING

100 g (3½ oz) raw prawns (shrimp), peeled and deveined

100 g (3½ oz) fresh scallop meat, diced

1 bunch coriander (cilantro), finely chopped

30 g (1 oz) water chestnuts, finely chopped

1 tsp salt

½ tsp ground white pepper

½ tsp sesame oil

To make the filling, place a prawn on a chopping board and smash it with the side of a cleaver to smash it. Repeat with the remaining prawns. Gather up all the smashed prawns and finely chop into a paste, then transfer to a mixing bowl. Add the remaining filling ingredients and stir for a minute until well combined. Cover and marinate in the fridge for 1 hour.

Using the 'gold ingot' folding technique on page 176, fold your wrappers around the filling.

Line a large bamboo steamer basket with a round sheet of baking paper with a few holes punched in it (see note, page 12). Working in batches, place the dumplings in the steamer, being sure not to overcrowd the basket. Cover and steam over a wok of hot simmering water over medium–high heat for 8–10 minutes, until cooked.

Remove from the heat, dress each dumpling with XO sauce, garnish with fried shallots and serve immediately.

PORK XIAO LONG BAO

Hailed as the king of dumplings, these soupy buns from Shanghai's Jiading district will quite literally explode in your mouth. The name says it all – xiao long bao, meaning 'small basket bun' in Mandarin, describes the paper-thin wrapper that cradles a piping hot soup and pork mince filling. Eaten hot and dipped in Chinkiang black vinegar, they offer a beautifully balanced sweet and tangy bite.

MAKES 18

1 quantity Xiao long bao dough (page 163), divided into 18 pieces

Soy, vinegar and ginger dipping sauce (page 165), to serve

GINGER & SPRING ONION WATER

1 spring onion (scallion), white part only, sliced

2.5 cm (1 in) piece of ginger, julienned

1 tbsp Sichuan peppercorns

150 ml (5 fl oz) boiling water

FILLING

180 g (6½ oz) minced (ground) pork, 30% fat

½ tsp ground white pepper

1 tsp salt

1 tbsp light soy sauce

1 tsp sesame oil

200 g (7 oz) Jellied stock (page 172), cut into 5 mm (¼ in) cubes

1 tsp minced ginger

1 spring onion (scallion), green part only, finely sliced

Combine the ginger and spring onion water ingredients in a bowl and leave to infuse for 15 minutes. Pour the liquid through a sieve into a jug, discarding the solids.

To make the filling, place the pork, pepper, salt, soy sauce and sesame oil in a large bowl. Stir vigorously for 2–3 minutes, until the mixture becomes pasty. Add half the ginger and spring onion water and stir until fully absorbed, then stir in the rest until the mixture is soft and slightly wet. Add the jellied stock, ginger and spring onion and stir gently to combine. Keep cold in the fridge until ready to use.

Take a piece of your xiao long bao dough and roll it out flat into a thin wrapper, about 11 cm (4¼ in) in diameter. Place the wrapper in the palm of your hand, then scoop a heaped tablespoon of filling – about 20 g (¾ oz) – onto the centre of the wrapper. Fold and pinch the edges in an anti-clockwise movement to create pleats and a little vent hole in the centre (see page 175 for more instructions). Repeat with the remaining dough and filling.

Line a large bamboo steamer basket with a round sheet of baking paper with a few holes punched in it (see note, page 12). Working in batches, place the dumplings in the steamer, being sure not to overcrowd the basket. Cover and steam over a wok of hot simmering water over medium heat for 12 minutes, until cooked.

Serve immediately, with the dipping sauce.

CRAB & PORK XIAO LONG BAO

Crab is a delicacy across many Asian cultures, and is commonly paired with pork in dim sum dumplings. The rich, sweet flavour of crab is well worth the effort it takes to prepare and pull away the meat from the shells. Here we've given instructions for preparing the crab meat from whole, fresh crabs, but you could make things simpler by purchasing frozen, ready-prepared crab meat.

MAKES 18

1 quantity Xiao long bao dough (page 163), divided into 18 pieces

Soy, vinegar and ginger dipping sauce (page 165), to serve

CRAB MEAT FILLING

2 fresh crabs (one male, one female; see note), or 150 g (5½ oz) frozen crab meat, thawed

2 tbsp vegetable oil

1 tsp minced ginger

1 tbsp Shaoxing rice wine

½ tsp ground white pepper

PORK FILLING

180 g (6½ oz) minced (ground) pork, 30% fat

1 tsp salt

1 tsp white sugar

1 tsp minced ginger

1 tbsp light soy sauce

2 tbsp water

150 g (5½ oz) crab meat filling (from above)

200 g (7 oz) Jellied stock (page 172), set and cut into 5 mm (¼ in) cubes

First, prepare the crab meat filling. Clean the crabs thoroughly by giving them a good scrub, then place them upside down in a bamboo basket and steam for 15 minutes. Remove from the heat. Once they are cool enough to handle, crack the crabs open and scrape all the flesh, roe and tomalley (the orange fat inside the shell) onto a plate, keeping the flesh separate from the roe and tomalley. Heat the oil over medium–high heat, add the roe and tomalley and stir-fry for a minute to infuse the oil. Add the crab meat and ginger, stirring to mix well. Add the rice wine and pepper, stir for another minute, then pour into a heatproof bowl to cool down. Cover and chill in the fridge until ready to use.

To make the pork filling, place the pork, salt and sugar in a large bowl and stir vigorously using your hand or chopsticks for 2–3 minutes, until pasty. Add the ginger, soy sauce and water and stir for about 30 seconds, until fully absorbed. Gently stir in the crab meat mixture until combined. Lastly, add the jellied stock, stirring slowly and gently until well combined. Cover and chill in the fridge until ready to use.

Using the xiao long bao folding technique on page 175, fold your wrappers around the filling.

Line a large bamboo steamer basket with a round sheet of baking paper with a few holes punched in it (see note, page 12). Working in batches, place the dumplings in the steamer, being sure not to overcrowd the basket. Cover and steam over a wok of hot simmering water over medium–high heat for 12 minutes, until cooked.

Serve immediately, with the dipping sauce.

NOTE: We use both male and female crabs for their roe and tomalley in this recipe. If using live crabs, put them to sleep in the freezer for an hour before preparing.

These are a delight for mushroom lovers! Earthy wood ear mushrooms and fresh shiitake and enoki mushrooms take centre stage in this filling, which also features carrot, wombok and tofu to make a delicious vegetarian-friendly dumpling. These dumplings are the same shape as xiao long bao but they aren't soupy inside – but don't despair, they're still completely moreish.

VEGETARIAN BAO

MAKES 25

1.5 quantity Xiao long bao dough (page 163), divided into 25 pieces

Soy, vinegar and ginger dipping sauce (page 165), to serve

FILLING

2–3 dried wood ear mushrooms

1 tbsp vegetable oil

2 tsp minced ginger

3 garlic cloves, finely chopped

60 g (2 oz) firm tofu, cut into 5 mm (¼ in) cubes

30 g (1 oz) finely chopped carrot

1 tbsp light soy sauce

2 tsp sesame oil

1 tsp ground white pepper

50 g (1¾ oz) fresh shiitake mushrooms, finely chopped

30 g (1 oz) enoki mushrooms, cut in half, any big clumps loosened

50 g (1¾ oz) wombok (Chinese cabbage), finely chopped

To make the filling, soak the dried wood ear mushrooms in hot water for 1 hour to rehydrate. Then rinse, trim off the woody parts, and slice the flesh into thin strips and set aside.

Heat the vegetable oil in a wok over medium–high heat. Saute the ginger and garlic for about 30 seconds, until fragrant. Add the tofu, carrot and wood ear mushrooms and stir-fry for a minute. Add the soy sauce, sesame oil and pepper. Stir-fry for another minute, then transfer to a large bowl to cool completely.

Add the remaining vegetables to the cooled filling, stirring to mix well. Keep the filling in the fridge until you are ready to assemble.

Using the xiao long bao folding technique on page 175, fold your wrappers around the filling.

Line a large bamboo steamer basket with a round sheet of baking paper with a few holes punched in it (see note, page 12). Working in batches, place the dumplings in the steamer, being sure not to overcrowd the basket. Cover and steam over a wok of hot simmering water over medium–high heat for 8–10 minutes, until cooked.

Serve immediately, with the dipping sauce.

Pho Soup Dumplings

Pho may be the national dish of Vietnam, but it's beloved all over the world for being an ultimate comfort food. This recipe is inspired by the classic flavours in pho bo (beef pho): ginger, cloves, star anise and fish sauce.

MAKES 18

1 quantity Xiao long bao dough (page 163), divided into 18 pieces

GINGER AND SPRING ONION WATER

1 spring onion (scallion), white part only, sliced

2.5 cm (1 in) piece of ginger, julienned

1 tbsp Sichuan peppercorns

150 ml (5 fl oz) boiling water

FILLING

180 g (6½ oz) minced (ground) beef

1 tsp salt

½ tsp ground black pepper

½ tsp minced ginger

1 tbsp light soy sauce

2 tsp sesame oil

200 g (7 oz) Pho stock, jellied (see note, page 173), set and cut into 5 mm (¼ in) cubes

1 bunch coriander (cilantro), leaves finely chopped

1 bunch Thai basil, leaves finely chopped

TO SERVE (OPTIONAL)

hoisin sauce, lime wedges, red bird's eye chillies (sliced)

Combine the ginger and spring onion water ingredients in a bowl and leave to infuse for 15 minutes. Pour the liquid through a sieve into a jug, discarding the solids.

To make the filling, place the beef, salt, pepper, ginger, soy sauce and sesame oil in a large bowl. Using chopsticks, and working in one direction, stir vigorously for 2–3 minutes, until the mixture becomes pasty. Add half the ginger and spring onion water and stir until fully absorbed, then stir in the rest until the mixture is soft and slightly wet. Add the stock, coriander and basil, stirring gently to combine. Cover and chill in the fridge until ready to use.

Using the xiao long bao folding technique on page 175, fold your wrappers around the filling.

Line a large bamboo steamer basket with a round sheet of baking paper with a few holes punched in it (see note, page 12). Working in batches, place the dumplings in the steamer, being sure not to overcrowd the basket. Cover and steam over a wok of hot simmering water over medium–high heat for 12 minutes, until cooked.

Serve immediately, with hoisin sauce, lime wedges and sliced fresh chilli, if desired.

CRAB TANG BAO

At double the size of your standard soup dumpling, this popular variation of the traditional Pork xiao long bao (page 18) proves that bigger really is better. The giant dumplings from Shanghai's Nanxiang town are stuffed with sweet crab meat and a rich, savoury soup that you can slurp up after biting open the skin.

MAKES 4 BIG DUMPLINGS

300 g (10½ oz) Jellied stock (page 172)

1 quantity Xiao long bao dough (page 163)

CRAB MEAT FILLING

300 g (10½ oz) fresh mud crab meat (from approx. 2 mud crabs), or 300 g (10½ oz) frozen crab meat, thawed

2 tbsp vegetable oil

3 ginger slices

1 tbsp brandy (optional)

½ tsp salt

½ tsp white sugar

pinch of ground white pepper

First, prepare the crab meat filling. Clean the crabs thoroughly by giving them a good scrub, then place them upside down in a bamboo basket and steam for 15 minutes. Remove from the heat. Once they are cool enough to handle, crack the crabs open and scrape all the flesh, roe (if using female crabs) and tomalley (the orange fat inside the shell) onto a plate, keeping them separate.

Heat the vegetable oil over medium–high heat. Fry the ginger slices for a minute to infuse the oil, then discard the ginger. Add the crab roe and tomalley and stir-fry for a minute to break up the bigger pieces. Stir in the crab meat, mixing well. Add the brandy (if using), salt, sugar and pepper, stir-fry for another minute, then transfer to a heatproof bowl to cool completely. Cover and chill in the fridge until ready to use.

Remove the top layer of fat from your jellied stock, if there is one, then finely chop the jelly. Keep it wrapped in the fridge until ready to use.

Cut out four sheets of baking paper, each a 25 cm (10 in) square. Cut the xiao long bao dough into four 45 g (1½ oz) portions. Roll each piece into a thin wrapper, about 18–20 cm (7–8 in) in diameter. Place the wrappers on the sheets of baking paper.

Mix together about 70 g (2½ oz) of the crab meat filling and 70 g (2½ oz) of the jellied stock. Place it in the centre of a wrapper. Slowly wrap it up into a large dumpling, using the xiao long bao folding technique on page 175. Repeat with the remaining filling and wrappers.

Working in batches, place one large dumpling in a small bamboo basket lined with a round sheet of baking paper punched with holes (see note, page 12). Cover and steam over a wok of hot simmering water over medium heat for 10–12 minutes, until cooked.

Remove from the heat. To serve, place a straw into the steam hole in the top of the dumpling to drink the soup with. Serve immediately.

KU CHAI KUEH

Combine the words ku chai (or koo chai), meaning chives in Hokkien and Teochew dialects, and kueh (or kuih), meaning 'dumpling' in Malay and Indonesian dialects, and you get this classic chive dumpling. While regional variations have developed over time, the soft translucent skin and bright green chive and dried shrimp filling are a mainstay. Serve these as they are or with a chilli sauce of your choice.

MAKES 30

- 30 Crystal dumpling wrappers (page 162), made with tapioca starch instead of potato starch
- Sichuan red chilli oil (page 166) or Thai sweet chilli sauce (page 168), to serve

FILLING

- 30 g (1 oz) dried shrimp
- 2 tbsp vegetable oil
- 5 garlic cloves, minced
- 300 g (10½ oz) garlic chives, cut into 1 cm (½ in) lengths
- 1 tsp salt
- ½ tsp ground white pepper
- 2 tsp sesame oil

To make the filling, first soak the dried shrimp in hot water for 30 minutes. Drain, then finely chop and set aside.

Heat the vegetable oil in a wok over medium heat, then saute the garlic and dried shrimp until the garlic is golden and crispy, about 2 minutes. Turn off the heat, add the garlic chives and stir-fry using the wok's residual heat until slightly softened. Stir in the salt, pepper and sesame oil, then set aside to cool completely.

Using the gyoza folding technique on page 177, fold your wrappers around the filling.

Line a large bamboo steamer basket with a round sheet of baking paper with a few holes punched in it (see note, page 12). Working in batches, place the dumplings in the steamer, being sure not to overcrowd the basket. Cover and steam over a wok of hot simmering water over medium–high heat for 7–8 minutes, until cooked. Serve immediately.

LAMB MOMOS

As cute as their name suggests, momos are a beloved street food snack introduced to Nepal by Tibetan immigrants. The lamb mince is marinated in a fragrant blend of cumin, turmeric, coriander and chilli, setting these dumplings apart from their Chinese counterparts. Whether steamed or fried, momos are typically served with achar (a spicy tomato dipping sauce).

MAKES 20

20 Basic dumpling wrappers (page 162)

Tomato achar (page 169), to serve

FILLING

150 g (5½ oz) minced (ground) lamb

½ onion, finely chopped

1 tbsp coriander (cilantro) leaves, finely chopped

1 spring onion (scallion), finely sliced

1 bird's eye chilli, finely chopped

1 tbsp vegetable oil

2 tbsp water

MARINADE

2 garlic cloves, finely chopped

1 tsp minced ginger

2 tsp dark soy sauce

1 tsp salt

1 tsp chilli powder

1 tsp ground cumin

½ tsp ground turmeric

½ tsp ground black pepper

¼ tsp ground nutmeg

To make the filling, place the lamb, onion, coriander, spring onion and chilli in a large bowl. Add all the marinade ingredients and mix together with your hand until well combined. Add the vegetable oil and continue to mix for another minute. Add the water and keep mixing until it is fully absorbed; the mixture should be sticky but not wet. Cover and marinate in the fridge for at least 1 hour, or overnight.

Using the gyoza folding technique on page 177, fold your wrappers around the filling.

Line a large bamboo steamer basket with a round sheet of baking paper with a few holes punched in it (see note, page 12). Working in batches, place the dumplings in the steamer, being sure not to overcrowd the basket. Cover and steam over a wok of hot simmering water over medium–high heat for 10–12 minutes, until cooked.

Serve immediately, with the tomato achar.

VEGETABLE MOMOS

Hindu diets in Nepal and India gave rise to the vegetarian momo. Instead of minced meat, these dumplings are filled with a mix of veggies, including cabbage and carrots, plus tofu. Paired with the same tomato achar as the Lamb momos (page 30), vegetarian momos offer the perfect balance of sweetness and spice in one bite.

MAKES 17

17 Basic dumpling wrappers (page 162)

Tomato achar (page 169), to serve

FILLING

1 tbsp vegetable oil

2 garlic cloves, finely chopped

1 tsp finely chopped ginger

1 bird's eye chilli, finely chopped

100 g (1⅓ cups) shredded cabbage

80 g (2¾ oz) shredded carrot

50 g (1¾ oz) firm tofu, crumbled and patted dry

2 spring onions (scallions), finely sliced

1 bunch coriander (cilantro), finely chopped

1 tbsp light soy sauce

1 tsp white sugar

1 tsp ground black pepper

½ tsp salt

To make the filling, heat the vegetable oil in a frying pan over medium–high heat and saute the garlic, ginger and chilli for about 15 seconds, until fragrant. Add the cabbage and carrot and stir-fry for 2–3 minutes, until softened. Add the tofu, spring onion, coriander, soy sauce, sugar, pepper and salt, then stir-fry for another 1–2 minutes, until most of the liquid has evaporated. Taste and adjust the seasonings accordingly. Remove from the heat and leave to cool to room temperature.

Using the gyoza folding technique on page 177, fold your wrappers around the filling.

Line a large bamboo steamer basket with a round sheet of baking paper with a few holes punched in it (see note, page 12). Working in batches, place the dumplings in the steamer, being sure not to overcrowd the basket. Cover and steam over a wok of hot simmering water over medium–high heat for 8–10 minutes, until cooked.

Serve immediately, with the tomato achar.

PORK MANDU

Mandu, more casually known as Korean dumplings, are traditionally prepared and enjoyed by families during the Korean Lunar New Year (Seollal). When meat is the main ingredient, they're known as gogi mandu, symbolising good luck and prosperity for the year ahead. Mandu are most commonly steamed or boiled, but can also be fried to a golden crisp.

MAKES 20

20 Basic dumpling wrappers (page 162)

Yangnyeom jang (page 171), to serve

FILLING

100 g (3½ oz) wombok (Chinese cabbage), finely chopped

1 tsp salt

40 g (1½ oz) Korean glass noodles

150 g (5½ oz) minced (ground) pork, 30% fat

15 g (½ oz) garlic chives

2 spring onions (scallions), finely sliced

1 tsp minced ginger

1 tbsp soy sauce

1 tbsp mirin

2 tsp sesame oil

½ tsp ground white pepper

To make the filling, place the cabbage in a bowl, sprinkle with the salt and toss together. Leave to sit for 30 minutes, then squeeze out all the excess liquid and set aside.

Boil the glass noodles in a saucepan of water over medium–high heat for 5–6 minutes, until cooked. Drain and rinse under cold running water, then finely chop the noodles into tiny pieces.

In a large bowl, combine the pork, cabbage, noodles, garlic chives and spring onion, mixing well. Add the remaining ingredients and stir for 1–2 minutes, until everything is well incorporated. The mixture should be sticky but not wet.

Using the gyoza folding technique on page 177, fold your wrappers around the filling.

Line a large bamboo steamer basket with a round sheet of baking paper with a few holes punched in it (see note, page 12). Working in batches, place the dumplings in the steamer, being sure not to overcrowd the basket. Cover and steam over a wok of hot simmering water over medium–high heat for 7–8 minutes, until cooked.

Serve immediately, with the dipping sauce.

HOBAK MANDU

Six ingredients are all you need to make the filling for these simple vegetarian dumplings, which are a summer staple at Korean Buddhist temples. Rooted in Buddhist principles, this filling omits pungent veggies like garlic and onions, instead relying on the natural sweetness of zucchini and the earthy depth of mushrooms for flavour.

MAKES 16

16 Basic dumpling wrappers (page 162)

Yangnyeom jang (page 171), to serve

FILLING

3 dried shiitake mushrooms

1 tbsp light soy sauce

2 tsp sesame oil

200 g (7 oz) zucchini (courgette), shredded

1 tsp salt

70 g (2½ oz) firm tofu, crumbled

To make the filling, soak the dried shiitake mushrooms in hot water for 1 hour to rehydrate. Squeeze the mushrooms to remove the liquid, then finely chop them. Place in a bowl with the soy sauce and 1 teaspoon of the sesame oil, stirring to mix well.

Place the zucchini in a bowl, sprinkle with the salt and toss together. Leave to sit for 15 minutes, then gently squeeze to remove some of the excess liquid. Set aside.

Heat the remaining sesame oil in a frying pan over medium–high heat. Saute the zucchini and tofu for 2–3 minutes, until the zucchini is slightly cooked and dry. Transfer to a mixing bowl.

Add the mushrooms to the pan and saute for about 1 minute, adding a spoonful of water if it gets too dry. Transfer the mushroom to the bowl with the zucchini mixture. Leave to cool to room temperature.

Using the gyoza folding technique on page 177, fold your wrappers around the filling.

Line a large bamboo steamer basket with a round sheet of baking paper with a few holes punched in it (see note, page 12). Working in batches, place the dumplings in the steamer, being sure not to overcrowd the basket. Cover and steam over a wok of hot simmering water over medium–high heat for 7–8 minutes, until cooked.

Serve immediately, with the dipping sauce.

TEOCHEW DUMPLINGS

Teochew dumplings or chiu zhao fun guo, hail from the Teochew (or Chaoshan) region in Guangdong province, China. Sharing the same crystal wrapper as Har gow (page 14) dumplings, these half-moon-shaped dumplings have a distinct crunch, thanks to the celery and roasted peanuts. Half the fun is trying to secure your chopsticks around the sticky skin.

MAKES 20

20 Crystal dumpling wrappers (page 162)

vegetable oil, for pan-frying

FILLING

100 g (3½ oz) minced (ground) pork, 30% fat

1 tsp light soy sauce

½ tsp caster (superfine) sugar

½ tsp cornflour (corn starch)

¼ tsp sesame oil

¼ tsp ground white pepper

2 dried shiitake mushrooms

20 g (¾ oz) dried shrimp

2 French shallots, finely chopped

25 g (1 oz) preserved radish, washed and finely chopped (see note)

10 g (¼ oz) pork fat, finely chopped

150 g (5½ oz) jicama, peeled and finely diced (see note, page 44)

40 g (1½ oz) celery, finely chopped

Ingredients continue over page →

To make the filling, place the pork in a bowl with the soy sauce, sugar, cornflour, sesame oil and pepper. Cover and marinate in the fridge for at least 1 hour.

Meanwhile, soak the dried shiitake mushrooms in hot water for 1 hour to rehydrate, and soak the dried shrimp in a separate bowl of hot water for 30 minutes. Drain the mushrooms, reserving 125 ml (½ cup) of the mushroom soaking water, then finely chop and set aside. Drain the dried shrimp, finely dice and set aside.

To prepare the seasoning mix, combine the sugar, oyster sauce, soy sauce, pepper, five spice and rice wine in a small bowl. In a separate bowl, mix the cornflour with the reserved mushroom soaking water to make a smooth slurry.

Heat 1 tablespoon of vegetable oil in a frying pan over medium–high heat. Add the shallot and stir-fry for about 1 minute, until golden. Add the preserved radish and chopped shiitake mushroom and stir-fry for 30 seconds. Add the dried shrimp and stir-fry for another 2 minutes, or until fragrant. Transfer the mixture to a bowl and set aside.

In the same pan, heat another 2 teaspoons of oil. Add the pork fat and stir-fry for 30 seconds to render some of the fat. Add the marinated pork and stir-fry for about 1 minute, until cooked. Return the sauteed radish and mushroom mixture to the pan, add the jicama and celery and stir everything together for 30 seconds.

1 bunch coriander (cilantro), leaves finely chopped

30 g (1 oz) garlic chives, finely sliced

1 tsp sesame oil

20 g (¾ oz) roasted salted peanuts

SEASONING MIX

1 tsp caster (superfine) sugar

2 tsp oyster sauce

1 tsp light soy sauce

½ tsp ground white pepper

½ tsp five spice powder

2 tsp Shaoxing rice wine

1 tbsp cornflour (corn starch)

Add the seasoning mix to the frying pan, then cover and cook for 1 minute, until most of the liquid has evaporated. Add the cornflour slurry, a little at a time, and keep stirring until the mixture is thick. Turn the heat off, stir in the coriander, garlic chives, sesame oil and peanuts until well combined, then set aside to cool completely.

Using the gyoza folding technique on page 177, fold your wrappers around the filling.

Line a large bamboo steamer basket with a round sheet of baking paper with a few holes punched in it (see note, page 12). Working in batches, place the dumplings in the steamer, being sure not to overcrowd the basket. Cover and steam over a wok of hot simmering water over medium–high heat for 10 minutes, until cooked. Serve immediately.

NOTE: Preserved radish can be found at any Asian supermarket. We are using the 'salty' version for this recipe.

1. Prawn crystal flower dumplings (page 42)

DUMPLINGS   2. Pho soup dumplings (page 24)   3. Teochew dumplings (page 38)   **41**

PRAWN CRYSTAL FLOWER DUMPLINGS

Pretty in pink, these steamed dumplings are a fancy twist on the classic prawn Har gow (page 14). The crystal wrappers are naturally coloured with red cabbage and carefully pleated to resemble cherry blossom petals. They're almost too pretty to eat – well, almost!

MAKES ABOUT 20

FILLING

350 g (12½ oz) raw prawn (shrimp) meat

60 g (2 oz) finely diced carrot (with some reserved for garnishing)

2 tsp sesame oil

1 tsp fish sauce

1 tsp salt

1 tsp ground white pepper

Ingredients continue over page →

To prepare the filling, place 200 g (7 oz) of the prawn meat in a blender and blitz into a paste. Cut the remaining prawn meat into small pieces and place in a bowl with the prawn paste. Add the remaining filling ingredients and mix everything together until well combined. Cover and marinate in the fridge for 1–2 hours.

To make the wrapper dough, place the cabbage and water in a saucepan and bring to a simmer over medium heat. Simmer for about 5 minutes, until the water turns purple. Pour the purple liquid into a heatproof bowl through a sieve. Add the lemon juice to turn the liquid pink.

Mix the wheat starch and salt together in a large mixing bowl. Reheat the pink liquid in the pan until simmering, then pour it over the wheat starch and stir to form a rough dough. Tip the dough out onto a work surface and flatten it slightly. Smear the lard over the dough, then knead it in. Keep kneading for 2–3 minutes, until you have a smooth dough. Wrap the dough and leave to rest for 10 minutes.

Roll the dough into a long log about 2.5 cm (1 in) thick, then cut the dough into 25 g (1 oz) portions. Place in a bowl and keep them covered with a damp cloth so the dough doesn't dry out.

Using the palm of your hand, slightly flatten a piece of dough, then use a rolling pin and roll it out into a thin wrapper, about 12 cm (4¾ in) in diameter. Put 1 tablespoon of the filling in the centre of the wrapper. Imagine the wrapper as a clockface. Starting at 2 o'clock, fold and pinch together the edges of the wrapper towards the centre. The sealed edges should look like a straight line coming from the centre of the dumpling. Repeat this folding and pinching action again at the 5, 7, 10 and 12 o'clock points, to make five petals with a tiny vent hole in the middle. The dumpling should look like a starfish shape.

PINK WRAPPER DOUGH

100 g (3½ oz) red cabbage, cut into thick slices

300 ml (10 fl oz) water

1 tbsp lemon juice

300 g (10½ oz) wheat starch

½ tsp salt

15 g (½ oz) lard

Take one petal and, starting from the centre, pinch and squeeze the top edge with your fingertips to make ridges along the edge. Join the bottom of the petal to the centre of the next petal by pinching them together, then repeat this process until all five petals are connected to resemble a flower.

Repeat using the remaining filling and wrappers. Place a few tiny cubes of carrot in the centre of each dumpling as a garnish.

Line a large bamboo steamer basket with a round sheet of baking paper with a few holes punched in it (see note, page 12). Working in batches, place the dumplings in the steamer, being sure not to overcrowd the basket. Cover and steam over a wok of hot simmering water over high heat for 7–8 minutes, until cooked. Serve immediately.

NOTE: These showstopping dumplings are a bit more fiddly to fold. There are videos online that can help you out if you get stuck, or feel free to use one of the other folding techniques at the back of the book (see pages 174–177).

CHAI KUEH

It's all about the crunch in these chewy crystal dumplings, sold by kueh stalls found at local markets, hawker centres and on street corners around Southeast Asia. The jicama-based filling gives chai kueh a lighter and slightly sweeter taste than Ku chai kueh (page 29), making them an easy breakfast or quick snack.

MAKES 16

16 Crystal dumpling wrappers (page 162)

FILLING

30 dried shrimp

60 ml (¼ cup) vegetable oil

3 garlic cloves, minced

300 g (10½ oz) jicama (see note), peeled and shredded

100 g (3½ oz) shredded carrot

2 tsp salt

1 tsp ground white pepper

Soak the dried shrimp in hot water for 30 minutes. Drain and rinse, then finely chop and set aside.

Heat the vegetable oil in a wok over medium–high heat. Add the garlic and stir-fry for about 30 seconds, until fragrant. Add the dried shrimp and stir-fry for another 30 seconds. Add the jicama and carrot and stir-fry for another 5 minutes, or until the vegetables have softened and most of the liquid has evaporated. Season with the salt and pepper, stirring to mix well. Remove from the heat to leave to cool completely.

Using the gyoza folding technique on page 177, fold your wrappers around the filling.

Line a large bamboo steamer basket with a round sheet of baking paper with a few holes punched in it (see note, page 12). Working in batches, place the dumplings in the steamer, being sure not to overcrowd the basket. Cover and steam over a wok of hot simmering water over medium–high heat for 7–8 minutes, until cooked. Serve immediately.

NOTE: Jicama or yam bean usually can be found in Asian supermarkets. Alternatively, you can substitute it with water chestnuts or turnip.

Adding sweet potato to the dumpling wrapper dough brings a beautiful golden colour and a lovely chewiness to these dumplings. The chicken filling is simply seasoned with coriander, garlic and soy sauce, proving that sometimes the simplest fillings can be the most satisfying!

SWEET POTATO CHICKEN & DUMPLINGS

MAKES 40

FILLING

500 g (1 lb 2 oz) minced (ground) chicken

1 egg

3 tbsp finely chopped coriander (cilantro) leaves

2 garlic cloves, minced

2 tbsp light soy sauce

1 tbsp dark soy sauce

1 tbsp cornflour (corn starch)

1 tsp ground white pepper

1 tbsp sesame oil

SWEET POTATO DOUGH

1 × 300 g (10½ oz) sweet potato, skin on

300 g (10½ oz) plain (all-purpose) flour, plus extra for dusting

1 tsp salt

Place all the filling ingredients in a large mixing bowl. Stir vigorously for 3–5 minutes, until the mixture is sticky and pasty, but not wet. Cover and refrigerate for 1 hour.

Meanwhile, prepare the dough. Preheat the oven to 180ºC (350ºF) and line a baking tray with baking paper. Place the sweet potato on the baking tray and roast for 30–35 minutes, until soft. Remove from the oven and, while still hot, carefully peel and mash the sweet potato in a bowl. Add the flour and salt and stir until combined. Knead the mixture into a rough dough, then cover and leave to rest for 10 minutes.

Knead the dough in the bowl for 1 minute, until soft and well combined. Transfer the dough to a floured work surface, then roll into a long log, about 2.5 cm (1 in) thick, and cut into four equal portions. Cut each portion into eight equal smaller pieces, each weighing 9–10 g (¼ oz). Cover the dough pieces, or put them in a container to stop them drying out while you fill the dumplings.

Using the palm of your hand, slightly flatten a piece of dough, then use a rolling pin and roll it out into a thin wrapper, about 8–10 cm (3¼–4 in) in diameter. Repeat with the remaining dough pieces.

Using the gyoza folding technique on page 177, fold your wrappers around the filling.

Line a large bamboo steamer basket with a round sheet of baking paper with a few holes punched in it (see note, page 12). Working in batches, place the dumplings in the steamer, being sure not to overcrowd the basket. Cover and steam over a wok of hot simmering water over high heat for 7–8 minutes, until cooked. Serve immediately.

DUMPLINGS

BANH IT TRAN

Loosely translating to 'naked little cake', these glutinous dumplings are a delicacy native to central Vietnam. The name reflects the simplicity of their minimalistic appearance – they are lightly drizzled with onion oil and served at room temperature with a zesty nuoc cham dipping sauce.

MAKES 13

vegetable oil, for cooking

1 spring onion (scallion), green part only, finely sliced and mixed with 2 tbsp vegetable oil, for garnishing

Nuoc cham (page 167), to serve

FILLING

100 g (3½ oz) split yellow mung beans (moong dal)

300 ml (10 fl oz) water

¼ tsp salt

50 g (1¾ oz) dried shrimp

1 garlic clove, crushed

1½ tsp white sugar

1 tsp chicken stock powder

1 French shallot, finely chopped

150 g (5½ oz) minced (ground) pork, 30% fat

½ tsp ground white pepper

120 g (4½ oz) raw prawn (shrimp) meat, cut into small pieces

Ingredients continue over page →

To prepare the filling, wash the mung beans several times under cold running water until the water runs clear, then soak them in water for 2 hours. Drain the mung beans and place them in a saucepan with the water and salt, then bring to a simmer over medium heat. Using a ladle, scoop off any froth on top. Once simmering, put the lid on, reduce the heat to low and cook for 20 minutes, at this point the mung beans should be dry-ish and mushy.

Meanwhile, soak the dried shrimp in hot water for 30 minutes. Drain and set aside.

Heat 1 teaspoon of vegetable oil in a frying pan over medium–high heat. Stir-fry the dried shrimp and the garlic for about 2 minutes, until the mixture is fragrant and the shrimp is slightly toasted. Remove from the heat, stir in ½ teaspoon of the sugar and the stock powder until well combined, then leave to cool to room temperature.

Transfer the cooled shrimp mixture to a blender and blitz into fine crumbs. Reserve 1 tablespoon for garnishing the dumplings.

In the same frying pan, heat another 1 tablespoon of oil over medium–high heat. Add the shallot and stir-fry for about 1 minute, until golden. Add the pork, stir, then cook for another minute. Add the remaining 1 teaspoon of sugar, ½ teaspoon of stock powder and the pepper and stir for about 2 minutes, or until the pork is fully cooked and most of the liquid has evaporated.

Add the prawn meat and stir-fry for a further 1 minute, until just cooked through, then remove from the heat. Stir in the cooked mung beans and dried shrimp crumbs, mixing well. Take a heaped tablespoon of the filling – about 35 g (1¼ oz) – and roll it into a ball. Repeat with the remaining filling, then cover until ready to be used.

STEAMED

DOUGH

400 g (14 oz) glutinous rice flour

½ tsp salt

1 tbsp white sugar

200 ml (7 fl oz) boiling water

125 ml (½ cup) water, at room temperature

To make the dough, place the rice flour, salt and sugar in a large heatproof bowl, stirring to mix well. While stirring continuously, pour in the hot water in a steady stream. Add half the room-temperature water and stir until fully absorbed, then add the remaining water and mix well. Using your hand, knead the mixture until it all comes together to form a dough. Wrap in plastic wrap and refrigerate for 30 minutes.

Knead the dough for 3–4 minutes until smooth, then keep it wrapped up to stop it drying out.

Tear off a small piece of dough – about 45 g (1½ oz) – and roll it into a ball. Press a dent in the centre with your thumb, then gradually stretch the dough out to make a cup. Place a ball of filling in the cup, gather the dough around, then gradually wrap up and seal. Roll the dough into a ball, then flatten slightly to make a round puck. Repeat with the remaining dough and filling.

Line a large bamboo steamer basket with a round sheet of baking paper with a few holes punched in it (see note, page 12). Working in batches, place the dumplings in the steamer, being sure not to overcrowd the basket. Cover and steam over a wok of hot simmering water over medium heat for 15 minutes, until cooked.

Remove from the heat. Brush the dumplings with some of the spring onion oil to prevent them from sticking together.

Serve the dumplings at room temperature, garnished with the spring onion and reserved dried shrimp crumbs, and with the nuoc cham on the side as a dipping sauce.

DUMPLINGS   Pictured overleaf

50 1. Saku sai moo (page 52) STEAMED

DUMPLINGS 2. Banh it tran (page 48)

SAKU SAI MOO

This popular golf ball–sized snack will disappear in just one bite. Commonly found at street food stalls and markets throughout Thailand, especially in Bangkok, the tapioca pearls are wrapped around a filling of caramelised pork, sweet pickled radish and crunchy roasted peanuts. This creates a delightful contrast to the chewy tapioca skin.

MAKES 14

banana leaves (see note, page 159), or baking paper, for steaming

GARLIC OIL

125 ml (½ cup) vegetable oil

1 garlic bulb, cloves finely sliced

FILLING

3 garlic cloves, peeled

1 bunch coriander (cilantro), roughly chopped

2 tsp ground black pepper

250 g (9 oz) minced (ground) pork, 30% fat

4–5 French shallots, finely chopped

50 g (1¾ oz) sweet preserved radish (see note, page 39), rinsed twice and finely diced

100 g (3½ oz) palm sugar, crushed into small pieces

2 tsp fish sauce

¼ tsp salt

¼ tsp ground white pepper

70 g (2½ oz) crushed roasted peanuts

Ingredients continue over page →

To prepare the garlic oil, warm the vegetable oil in a frying pan over medium heat. Add the garlic and stir-fry for about 5 minutes, until light golden brown. Pour the oil through a fine sieve into a heatproof bowl and leave to drain. Reserve the fried garlic for garnishing the dumplings, and set the oil aside.

To make the filling, use a mortar and pestle to pound and grind the garlic, coriander and black pepper into a paste. Heat 1 tablespoon of the garlic oil in a frying pan over medium–high heat, then stir-fry the garlic paste for about 30 seconds, until fragrant. Add the pork, breaking up any big lumps into small pieces, and stir-fry for 2–3 minutes, until fully cooked. Transfer the mixture to a bowl and set aside.

In the same pan, heat another tablespoon of garlic oil over medium–high heat. Stir-fry the shallot and radish for about 1 minute, until the shallot is soft and translucent. Add the palm sugar, reduce the heat to low and keep stirring for 4–5 minutes, until all the sugar has caramelised and has turned dark brown.

Return the pork mixture to the pan and stir-fry for 3–4 minutes, until most of the liquid has evaporated. Stir in the fish sauce, salt and pepper, mixing well. Add the peanuts and stir-fry for another minute or two, until the mixture is dry and sticky. Transfer to a bowl to cool completely.

TAPIOCA PEARLS

400 g (14 oz) packet small tapioca pearls

750 ml (3 cups) water

TO SERVE

1 head of green leaf lettuce, washed, leaves separated

1 large red chilli, finely sliced

1 bunch coriander (cilantro), sprigs separated

Meanwhile, prepare the tapioca pearls. Place the tapioca in a large bowl, add the water and leave to soak for 20 minutes. Drain the tapioca through a sieve and set aside for 15–20 minutes to remove any excess water.

Grab a tablespoonful of the cooled filling and roll it into a 2.5 cm (1 in) ball. Repeat with the remaining filling.

Gather a tablespoon of tapioca pearls in your hand, roughly roll into a ball, then flatten into a thin disc. Place a ball of filling in the centre, then gently wrap the tapioca pearls around it and roll it into a golf ball–sized ball. Patch up any gaps with extra tapioca pearls. Place on a tray and repeat with the remaining ingredients.

Line a bamboo steamer with a banana leaf, then brush the banana leaf with some of the garlic oil. You could also use a round piece of baking paper with holes punched in it (see note, page 12).

Working in batches, place the dumpling balls in the steamer, being sure not to overcrowd the basket. Cover and steam over a wok of hot simmering water over medium heat for 8–10 minutes, until cooked.

Once steamed, brush each dumpling with garlic oil to stop them sticking. Transfer to a serving plate and sprinkle with the reserved fried garlic from the garlic oil.

Serve the dumplings as they are, or wrap them in lettuce leaves, with some sliced chilli and coriander sprigs.

DUMPLINGS   Pictured previous

FRIED PRAWN WONTONS

Wontons are truly one of the greatest bites of food to exist. When served during Lunar New Year, they symbolise wealth and good fortune due to their shape, which resemble gold ingots (widely used as currency during the Song, Yuan, Ming and Qing dynasties). Fried prawn wontons are especially popular in the Guangdong province – the heartland of Cantonese cuisine – and across southern China, where fresh seafood is easily accessible.

MAKES 20

20 Wonton wrappers (page 163)

vegetable oil, for frying

Thai sweet chilli sauce (page 168), to serve

FILLING

400 g (14 oz) raw prawn (shrimp) meat

2 tsp sesame oil

1 tsp fish sauce

1 tsp salt

1 tsp ground white pepper

To make the filling, place half the prawns in a blender and blitz into a paste. Transfer to a mixing bowl.

Chop the remaining prawns into small pieces and add to the prawn paste. Add the sesame oil, fish sauce, salt and pepper and stir until well combined.

Fill and shape the dumplings using the 'gold ingot' folding technique on page 176.

Half-fill a large saucepan or wok with vegetable oil and heat over medium–high heat. Test the oil is hot enough by dipping a wooden chopstick into it: if the oil fizzes, it is ready. Working in batches, carefully lower the dumplings into the hot oil and fry for 3–4 minutes, until golden brown, stirring occasionally. Transfer to a wire rack to drain off any excess oil.

Serve hot, with sweet chilli sauce.

PAN-FRIED PORK WONTONS

Crispy on the bottom and juicy on the inside, pan-fried pork wontons are an addictive Cantonese appetiser that have found a home on menus at Chinese restaurants around the world. Encased in thin wonton wrappers, these delicate pork dumplings are pan-fried until their bottoms turn just golden, then steamed to cook through and served immediately with soy or chilli sauce.

MAKES 20

- 20 Wonton wrappers (page 163)
- vegetable oil, for pan frying
- Sichuan red chilli oil (page 166), to serve
- soy sauce, to serve

FILLING

- 250 g (9 oz) minced (ground) pork, 30% fat
- 1 tbsp light soy sauce
- 1 tsp sesame oil
- ½ tsp salt
- pinch of ground white pepper
- 2 tbsp water
- 1 spring onion (scallion), finely sliced
- 2–3 garlic cloves, finely chopped
- 1 tbsp finely sliced coriander (cilantro) stems

To make the filling, place the pork, soy sauce, sesame oil, salt, pepper and water in a bowl. Using a pair of chopsticks or your hand, stir vigorously for 2–3 minutes, until the mixture resembles a sticky paste. Add the spring onion, garlic and coriander and stir until well combined. Cover and leave to rest in the fridge for at least 1 hour, preferably overnight.

Fill and shape the dumplings using the 'gold ingot' folding technique on page 176.

To pan-fry, heat about 1 tablespoon of vegetable oil in a non-stick frying pan over medium heat. Place as many dumplings in the pan as will fit in a single layer without touching each other. Cook for about 2 minutes, until the bottoms of the dumplings turn slightly brown. Pour 60 ml (¼ cup) water into the pan, cover with a lid and increase the heat to medium–high. Steam the dumplings for 3 minutes, or until most of the water has evaporated. Remove the lid. Drizzle 1 teaspoon of vegetable oil into the pan and shake the pan to dislodge the dumplings. Cook uncovered for another minute, or until the bottoms of the dumplings are crispy and golden brown. Remove from the pan and repeat to cook the remaining dumplings.

Serve hot, with your choice of dipping sauce.

HAM SUI GOK

Eating glutinous rice dumplings is the ultimate way to get your fried and chewy fix all in one bite. The name ham sui gok, meaning 'salty water dumplings', refers to the traditional cooking method of boiling the dumplings before frying them. The result is an unusually crisp yet chewy skin – subtly sweetened by sugar – contrasting the sticky, savoury filling of shrimp and shiitake mushrooms.

MAKES 12

vegetable oil, for frying

GLUTINOUS RICE DOUGH

225 g (8 oz) glutinous rice flour

40 g (1½ oz) caster (superfine) sugar

50 g (1¾ oz) pork lard, melted and at room temperature

180 ml (6 fl oz) cold water

85 g (3 oz) wheat starch

125 ml (½ cup) boiling water

Ingredients continue over page →

To make the dough, combine the glutinous rice flour and sugar in a large bowl, mixing well. Drizzle the lard over the flour while stirring to combine. Keep stirring while adding the cold water a little bit at a time until fully absorbed. Knead the mixture into a rough dough by hand, then cover.

Place the wheat starch in a heatproof bowl. Pour the hot water over, then stir into sticky crumbs. Cool slightly, then knead for about 1 minute into a smooth dough.

Tear the wheat dough into small chunks and add to the rice flour mixture. Tip all the dough mixture onto a work surface and knead for 1–2 minutes, until both doughs are well mixed together. Place a small piece of dough – about 50 g (1¾ oz) – in a heatproof bowl, cover and heat in the microwave for 30 seconds. Carefully embed the hot stretchy dough back into the remaining dough, folding and kneading them together for 2–3 minutes, until malleable and elastic. Wrap the dough in plastic wrap and leave to rest in the fridge for 1 hour.

Meanwhile, start making the filling. Soak the dried shrimp and shiitake mushrooms in separate bowls of hot water for 30 minutes, then drain. Finely chop the shrimp, finely dice the mushrooms and set aside separately.

Place the pork, cornflour, water and ½ teaspoon of the salt in a bowl. Stir to mix well, then set aside.

Heat the vegetable oil in a frying pan or wok over medium–high heat. Stir-fry the garlic and dried shrimp for about 30 seconds, until fragrant. Add the pork mixture and stir-fry for about 2 minutes, breaking up any big clumps. Add the shiitake and celery and stir-fry for another 30 seconds, then stir in the oyster sauce, soy sauce, pepper and remaining ½ teaspoon of salt, mixing well. Stir the cornflour slurry until smooth, then stir it through the pork mixture until well coated. Turn off the heat, stir in the sesame oil, spring onion and coriander and leave to cool completely.

FILLING

15 g (½ oz) dried shrimp

3–4 dried shiitake mushrooms

120 g (4½ oz) minced (ground) pork, 30% fat

1 tbsp cornflour (corn starch)

2 tbsp water

1 tsp salt

2 tbsp vegetable oil

2 garlic cloves, finely chopped

30 g (1 oz) celery, finely diced

1 tbsp oyster sauce

1 tbsp light soy sauce

½ tsp ground white pepper

1 tsp cornflour (corn starch), mixed with 2 tbsp water

1 tsp sesame oil

1 spring onion (scallion), finely sliced

1 tbsp finely sliced coriander (cilantro) stems

Take the dough out of the fridge 30 minutes before you want to start wrapping the dumplings, to make the dough workable again. Knead the dough a few times to soften it. Divide in half and roll each piece into two logs. Cut each log into six equal portions, about 40 g (1½ oz) each, to make 12 pieces.

To make the dumplings, roll a piece of dough into a ball. Flatten it into a circle, press your thumb in the centre to make an indentation, then gently stretch it out to form a small cup. Put a heaped spoonful of filling (about 15 g/½ oz) in the centre. Fold the dough over and pinch the edges together to seal, then roll the dumpling into the shape of a rugby ball. Repeat with the remaining dough and filling.

Half-fill a large saucepan or wok with vegetable oil and bring the oil temperature up to 160ºC (320ºF) over high heat. Test the oil temperature by dropping a small piece of dough into the hot oil; if the oil bubbles and the dough floats to the surface, it is ready.

Reduce the heat to low. Working in small batches, add the dumplings to the hot oil and keep stirring with wooden chopsticks to stop them sticking to each other. When the dumplings float to the surface, turn the heat back up to medium and fry for a further 15 minutes, or until golden brown, stirring continuously.

Transfer to a wire rack to drain off any excess oil. Leave to cool slightly before serving.

1. Hai choe (page 64)

DUMPLINGS 2. Ham sui gok (page 60) 63

HAI CHOE

Picture a meatball wrapped in bean curd skin. That's a simple way to describe hai choe before the crab meat roll is deep-fried until golden brown. While hai choe originated from China's Teochew region, it's now more popular in Bangkok and the coastal regions of Thailand, where fresh seafood is plentiful.

MAKES 20–25

- 2–3 large soft bean curd sheets (see note)
- vegetable oil, for frying
- 1 egg, beaten
- 120 g (1 cup) tapioca starch, for dusting
- Thai sweet chilli sauce (page 168), to serve

FILLING

- 150 g (5½ oz) raw prawns (shrimp), peeled and deveined
- 1 egg, beaten
- 100 g (3½ oz) minced (ground) pork, 30% fat
- 50 g (1¾ oz) pork fat, finely chopped
- 3–4 garlic cloves, finely chopped
- 1 tbsp finely chopped coriander (cilantro) stems
- 50 g (1¾ oz) water chestnuts, finely diced
- 1 tbsp cornflour (corn starch)

Ingredients continue over page →

To make the filling, place a prawn on a chopping board and, using the side of a cleaver, smash the meat into mush. One at a time, repeat with the remaining prawns. Gather up all the prawn meat and chop it into a fine paste. Put the prawn paste in a bowl with the egg, pork and pork fat, then massage and mix everything together. Add the remaining ingredients, except the crab meat. Mix for 1–2 minutes, until there are no more flour lumps and everything is well combined. Now stir in the crab meat, mixing well; the filling should be sticky but not wet. Cover and refrigerate for 1 hour.

Cut the bean curd sheets into 25 cm x 15 cm (10 in x 6 in) rectangles.

Place a bean curd sheet on a sushi mat, with the longest side facing you. Wipe it with a damp cloth to moisten it slightly. Leaving a 2.5 cm (1 in) gap on all sides, spread a roll of filling along the bottom edge of the sheet. Lift the sushi mat up and roll the sheet up tightly, making sure there are no air pockets in the filling. Using kitchen twine, tie knots on each end to seal, then tie knots at 2.5 cm (1 in) intervals along the roll – but not too tightly, so the sheet doesn't tear. Your roll should now look like a link of sausages. Repeat with the remaining filling and bean curd sheets.

Working in batches if needed, place the rolls in a large bamboo steamer basket lined with baking paper. Cover and steam over a wok of hot simmering water over medium heat for 20 minutes. Remove from the heat and cool completely to room temperature. Cut the rolls at the tied intervals into individual dumplings and discard the kitchen twine.

1 tbsp caster (superfine) sugar

1 tbsp Shaoxing rice wine

1 tbsp light soy sauce

2 tsp sesame oil

2 tsp salt

1 tsp Chinese five-spice

1 tsp ground white pepper

150 g (5½ oz) fresh crab meat (or thawed frozen crab meat)

Half-fill a large saucepan or wok with vegetable oil and heat over medium heat. Beat the egg in a bowl, and place the tapioca starch on a plate. Working in batches, dip the dumplings in the egg wash, then coat in the tapioca starch, dusting off any excess. Carefully lower the dumplings into the hot oil and fry for about 5 minutes, or until crispy and golden brown. Transfer to a wire rack to drain off any excess oil.

Serve hot, with sweet chilli sauce.

NOTE: Bean curd sheets are available at Asian supermarkets. We are using the soft bean curd sheets in this recipe, not the dried crispy ones.

THUNG THONG

Thung thong are a Thai twist on the Chinese fried wonton, easily recognisable by its signature shape that resembles – you guessed it – a money bag. True to its nickname, these crispy appetisers are exchanged during the Thai New Year (Songkran) to symbolise wishes for wealth and good fortune in the coming year.

MAKES 20

8–10 spring onions (scallions), green part only

5 spring roll wrappers (21 × 21 cm/8¼ × 8¼ in), cut into quarters (to yield 20 wrappers)

vegetable oil, for frying

Thai sweet chilli sauce (page 168), to serve

FILLING

120 g (4½ oz) minced (ground) pork, 30% fat

100 g (3½ oz) raw prawn (shrimp) meat, finely chopped

2 tsp light soy sauce

1 tsp sesame oil

1 tsp salt

½ tsp ground white pepper

100 g (3½ oz) water chestnuts, finely diced

Put the spring onions in a heatproof bowl, pour boiling water over and leave for about a minute, until the spring onions have softened. Drain, pat dry, then carefully cut each stalk lengthways into long thin strips. Set aside.

To make the filling, place the pork, prawn meat, soy sauce, sesame oil, salt and pepper in a bowl. Stir vigorously until the mixture is well combined and pasty, but not wet. Gently stir the water chestnuts through.

Spoon a tablespoon of filling into the centre of a spring roll wrapper. Gather all the edges together to form a small sack. Secure the top by tying it closed with a spring onion strip, trimming off the excess. Repeat with the remaining wrappers and filling.

Half-fill a large saucepan or wok with vegetable oil and heat over medium–high heat. Test the oil is hot enough by dipping a wooden chopstick into it: if the oil fizzes, it is ready. Working in batches, carefully lower the dumplings into the hot oil and fry for 3–4 minutes, until golden brown, stirring occasionally. Transfer to a wire rack to drain off any excess oil.

Serve hot, with sweet chilli sauce.

Spicy Thai-Style Beef Dumplings

These deep-fried wontons are packed with flavours that are common across Thailand and Southeast Asia: lemongrass, shallots, garlic, fish sauce and, of course, plenty of chilli.

MAKES 20

20 Wonton wrappers (page 163)

vegetable oil, for frying

Thai sweet chilli sauce (page 168), to serve

FILLING

2 garlic cloves, peeled

2 red bird's eye chillies, stems removed

2 cm (¾ in) piece of ginger, peeled

2 lemongrass stems, white part only

3 red Asian shallots or French shallots

60 ml (¼ cup) water

200 g (7 oz) minced (ground) beef

1 tbsp lime juice

2 tsp oyster sauce

2 tsp fish sauce

1 tsp brown sugar

1 tbsp cornflour (corn starch)

1 bunch coriander (cilantro), finely chopped

2 tsp sesame oil

To make the filling, place the garlic, chillies, ginger, lemongrass, shallot and water in a food processor and blend into a fine paste.

Place the beef and the spice paste in a large bowl and stir vigorously for 2 minutes, or until the mixture is well combined and slightly sticky. Add the lime juice, oyster sauce, fish sauce and sugar and mix well. Stir in the cornflour and mix until there are no flour lumps. Add the coriander and sesame oil and stir for another minute; the mixture should be sticky but not wet.

Fill and shape the dumplings using the 'gold ingot' folding technique on page 176.

Half-fill a large saucepan or wok with vegetable oil and heat over medium–high heat. Test the oil is hot enough by dipping a wooden chopstick into it: if the oil fizzes, it is ready. Working in batches, carefully lower the dumplings into the hot oil and fry for 3–4 minutes, until golden brown, stirring occasionally. Transfer to a wire rack to drain off any excess oil.

Serve hot, with sweet chilli sauce.

Pangsit Goreng

Pangsit goreng, which means 'fried dumplings' in Indonesian, is a go-to appetiser, often served alongside mains like nasi goreng (fried rice) or mie goreng (fried noodles). These crowd-pleasers are easy to prepare in bulk, making them perfect for parties, family gatherings and festive occasions.

MAKES 15

15 Wonton wrappers (page 163)

vegetable oil, for deep-frying

FILLING

250 g (9 oz) minced (ground) chicken

1 egg

2 garlic cloves, minced

1 spring onion (scallion), finely sliced

2 tsp sesame oil

1 tsp oyster sauce

1 tsp salt

1 tsp ground white pepper

1 tbsp cornflour (corn starch)

DIPPING SAUCE

50 ml (1¾ fl oz) hot water

3 tbsp sambal oelek

1 tbsp tomato ketchup

1 tsp white vinegar

1 tsp caster (superfine) sugar

To make the filling, place the chicken, egg, garlic and spring onion in a bowl and stir to combine. Add the sesame oil, oyster sauce, salt and pepper and stir to mix well. Add the cornflour and stir until there are no lumps. If the filling is still wet, mix in an extra teaspoon of cornflour at a time until the mixture is sticky. Cover and refrigerate for 1 hour.

Combine all the dipping sauce ingredients in a small bowl and stir until the sugar has dissolved. Taste and adjust the seasoning accordingly.

Fill and shape the dumplings using the 'gold ingot' folding technique on page 176.

Half-fill a large saucepan or wok with vegetable oil and heat over medium–high heat. Test the oil is hot enough by dipping a wooden chopstick into it: if the oil fizzes, it is ready. Working in batches, carefully lower the dumplings into the hot oil and fry for 3–4 minutes, until golden brown, stirring occasionally. Transfer to a wire rack to drain off any excess oil.

Serve hot, with the dipping sauce.

TRADITIONAL JAPANESE PORK GYOZAS

From street food stalls to sushi trains and upscale omakases, gyoza have become a comfort food enjoyed around the world. Inspired by traditional Chinese jiaozi dumplings, they were introduced to Japan by Chinese immigrants after World War II. Unlike jiaozi, which are simply boiled or steamed, gyoza are pan-fried on one side to achieve a crispy bottom. Pork remains the classic filling.

MAKES 16

16 Basic dumpling wrappers (page 162)

vegetable oil, for pan-frying

sesame oil, for drizzling

Soy, vinegar and ginger dipping sauce (page 165) or Yangnyeom jang (page 171), to serve

FILLING

180 g (6½ oz) cabbage, finely chopped

1 tsp salt

150 g (5½ oz) minced (ground) pork, 30% fat

20 g (¾ oz) garlic chives, finely chopped

2 garlic cloves, minced

1 spring onion (scallion), finely sliced

1 tsp minced ginger

2 tsp light soy sauce

2 tsp sake or mirin

1 tsp sesame oil

1 tsp caster (superfine) sugar

pinch of ground black pepper

To make the filling, toss the cabbage and salt in a bowl, mixing well. Leave to sweat for 30 minutes, then squeeze as much liquid out of the cabbage as possible. Add the remaining filling ingredients to the cabbage along with an extra pinch of salt, then stir until well combined.

Fill and shape the dumplings using the gyoza folding technique on page 177.

Heat about 1 tablespoon of vegetable oil in a non-stick frying pan over medium heat. Place as many dumplings in the pan as will fit in a single layer without touching each other. Cook for about 2 minutes, until the bottoms of the dumplings turn slightly brown. Pour 60 ml (¼ cup) water into the pan, cover with a lid and increase the heat to medium–high. Steam the dumplings for 3 minutes, or until most of the water has evaporated. Remove the lid. Drizzle 1 teaspoon of sesame oil into the pan and shake the pan to dislodge the dumplings. Cook uncovered for another minute, until the bottoms of the dumplings are crispy and golden brown. Remove from the pan and repeat to cook the remaining dumplings.

Serve hot, with your choice of dipping sauce.

PRAWN GYOZAS WITH CRISPY SKIRT

Dress your gyoza to impress with a crispy skirt – a modern technique that's sure to steal the show. Often called hanetsuki gyoza or gyoza with wings, this method involves pouring a flour slurry around the dumplings as they fry to extend the crunch around the edges. Flipping them in one piece is part of the fun!

MAKES 16

16 Basic dumpling wrappers (page 162)

vegetable oil, for pan-frying

2 tsp plain (all-purpose) flour, mixed with 125 ml (½ cup) water

Sichuan red chilli oil (page 166) or Crispy garlic chilli oil (page 165), to serve

FILLING

400 g (14 oz) raw prawn (shrimp) meat

25 g (1 oz) garlic chives, finely sliced

60 g (2 oz) water chestnuts, finely diced

1½ tbsp light soy sauce

1½ tbsp Shaoxing rice wine

1 tbsp sesame oil

2 tbsp cornflour (corn starch)

To make the filling, place half the prawn meat in a blender and blitz into a paste. Cut the remaining prawn meat in small pieces and place in a bowl with the prawn paste. Add the remaining filling ingredients and mix until well combined.

Fill and shape the dumplings using the gyoza folding technique on page 177.

In a large non-stick frying pan – at least 24 cm (9½ in) in diameter – heat about 2 tablespoons of vegetable oil over medium–low heat. Place as many dumplings in the pan as will fit in a single layer without touching each other. Give the flour slurry a quick stir and pour just enough to cover the base of the frying pan in a thin layer (you may not need it all), ensuring you do not pour it on the dumplings. Cover with a lid and cook for 7–8 minutes. Remove the lid and continue to cook for 2–3 minutes, until all the water has evaporated. During this time, tilt or rotate the pan ever so slightly, so a crispy 'skirt' forms in the pan, and all the dumplings cook evenly, with golden brown bottoms.

Turn off the heat and place an upside-down serving plate over the dumplings. While holding the plate and pan at the same time, flip the dumplings in one swift motion over onto the plate.

Repeat to cook the remaining dumplings. Serve hot, with your choice of chilli oil.

Crispy on the bottom but perfectly steamed through, potstickers get their name from the Cantonese word 'wor tip', meaning 'pot stick' in English. Using a non-stick frying pan will avoid that fate for these plump mushroom and tofu–filled dumplings!

TOFU & MUSHROOM POTSTICKERS

MAKES 20

20 Basic dumpling wrappers (page 162)

vegetable oil

sesame oil, for drizzling

Sichuan red chilli oil (page 166), to serve

FILLING

2–3 dried wood ear mushrooms

50 g (1¾ oz) fresh shiitake mushrooms

100 g (3½ oz) enoki mushrooms,

50 g (1¾ oz) shimeji mushrooms

1 tbsp vegetable oil

2 garlic cloves, minced

½ tsp minced ginger

200 g (7 oz) firm tofu, smashed and crumbled

1 tbsp light soy sauce

1 tsp dark soy sauce

pinch of ground white pepper

1 tsp sesame oil

1 tbsp cornflour (corn starch), mixed with 2 tbsp water

1 spring onion (scallion), finely sliced

1 bunch coriander (cilantro), finely chopped

To make the filling, soak the wood ear mushrooms in hot water for 1 hour to rehydrate. Rinse, trim off the woody parts, then slice the flesh into thin strips and set aside. Prepare the shiitake, enoki and shimeji mushrooms: dice the fresh shiitake mushrooms, cut the enoki mushrooms into 5 cm (2 in) lengths and halve then finely slice the shimeji mushrooms.

Heat the vegetable oil in a frying pan over medium–high heat. Saute the garlic and ginger for 30 seconds, or until fragrant. Add the tofu and all the mushrooms and cook for 3–4 minutes, until the mushrooms have softened, stirring occasionally. Add the soy sauces and pepper and stir-fry until well coated. Stir in the cornflour slurry until most of the liquid has evaporated and the mixture is slightly sticky. Turn off the heat and stir in the spring onion and coriander, mixing well. Set aside to cool completely.

Fill and shape the dumplings using the gyoza folding technique on page 177.

Heat about 1 tablespoon of oil in a non-stick frying pan over medium heat. Place as many dumplings in the pan as will fit in a single layer without touching each other. Cook for about 2 minutes, until the bottoms of the dumplings turn slightly brown. Pour 60 ml (¼ cup) water into the pan, cover with a lid and increase the heat to medium–high. Steam the dumplings for 3 minutes, or until most of the water has evaporated. Remove the lid. Drizzle 1 teaspoon of sesame oil into the pan and shake the pan to dislodge the dumplings. Cook uncovered for another minute, or until the bottoms of the dumplings are crispy and golden brown. Remove from the pan and repeat to cook the remaining dumplings.

Serve hot, with your choice of chilli oil.

WATER CHESTNUT & LEEK DUMPLINGS

These dumplings are satisfyingly crunchy. From the crispy pan-fried bottoms through to the vegetarian filling which is peppered with finely diced water chestnuts (aquatic tuber vegetables which are native to Southeast Asia and Southern China). You'll find it hard to stop at just one!

MAKES 20

20 Basic dumpling wrappers (page 162)

vegetable oil, for pan-frying

sesame oil, for drizzling

Sichuan red chilli oil (page 166), to serve

FILLING

250 g (9 oz) cabbage, shredded

1 tsp salt

2 tbsp vegetable oil

200 g (7 oz) leek, white part only, finely chopped

80 g (2¾ oz) water chestnuts, finely diced

1 tbsp light soy sauce

1 tsp salt

1 tsp caster (superfine) sugar

1 tsp ground white pepper

2 tbsp cornflour (corn starch), mixed with 60 ml (¼ cup) water

40 g (1½ oz) garlic chives, finely sliced

To make the filling, toss the cabbage and salt together in a bowl, mixing well. Leave to sweat for 10 minutes, then squeeze as much liquid out of the cabbage as possible. Set aside.

Heat the vegetable oil in a frying pan over medium–high heat. Stir-fry the cabbage for 1 minute, until soft. Add the leek and stir-fry for another minute, or until fragrant. Mix the water chestnuts through. Add the soy sauce, salt, sugar and pepper and stir-fry for about 30 seconds, until most of the liquid has evaporated. Give the cornflour slurry a quick stir and pour it into the pan, stirring until the mixture is thick and slightly sticky. Turn off the heat and thoroughly mix the garlic chives through. Transfer to a bowl to cool completely.

Fill and shape the dumplings using the gyoza folding technique on page 177.

Heat about 1 tablespoon of oil in a non-stick frying pan over medium heat. Place as many dumplings in the pan as will fit in a single layer without touching each other. Cook for about 2 minutes, until the bottoms of the dumplings turn slightly brown. Pour 60 ml (¼ cup) water into the pan, cover with a lid and increase the heat to medium–high. Steam the dumplings for 3 minutes, or until most of the water has evaporated. Remove the lid. Drizzle 1 teaspoon of sesame oil into the pan and shake the pan to dislodge the dumplings. Cook uncovered for another minute, until the bottoms of the dumplings are crispy and golden brown. Remove from the pan and repeat to cook the remaining dumplings.

Serve hot, with your choice of dipping sauce.

SICHUAN LAMB DUMPLINGS

Lamb is not commonly eaten in China's southern provinces, but in the north it is a staple. It is often paired with cumin and Sichuan pepper and can be served in stir-fries, as meat skewers, or in dumplings.

MAKES 30

30 Basic dumpling wrappers (page 162)

vegetable oil, for pan-frying

Soy, vinegar and ginger dipping sauce (page 165), to serve

Sichuan red chilli oil (page 166) or Crispy garlic chilli oil (page 165), to serve

FILLING

60 ml (¼ cup) vegetable oil

1 large onion, finely diced

3 garlic cloves, minced

2.5 cm (1 in) piece of ginger, grated

1 tbsp ground cumin

2 tsp Sichuan chilli flakes or gochugaru (Korean chilli flakes)

1 tsp ground Sichuan peppercorns

300 g (10½ oz) minced (ground) lamb

2 tbsp light soy sauce

2 tsp dark soy sauce

1 tbsp Shaoxing rice wine

1 tbsp cornflour (corn starch)

1 bunch coriander (cilantro), leaves finely chopped

To make the filling, heat the vegetable oil in a frying pan over medium–high heat and saute the onion for 1 minute, or until translucent. Add the garlic and ginger and stir-fry for another minute, or until fragrant. Add the cumin, chilli flakes and ground peppercorns and stir-fry for 30 seconds. Remove from the heat.

Put the lamb in a large bowl with the cooked spice mixture. Add the soy sauces, rice wine and cornflour. Stir vigorously for 2–3 minutes, until the mixture is sticky but not wet. Add the coriander leaves and mix well.

Fill and shape the dumplings using the gyoza folding technique on page 177.

Heat about 2 tablespoons of oil in a non-stick frying pan over medium heat. Place as many dumplings in the pan as will fit in a single layer without touching each other. Cook for about 2 minutes, until the bottoms of the dumplings turn slightly brown. Pour 60 ml (¼ cup) water into the pan, cover with a lid and increase the heat to medium–high. Steam the dumplings for 3 minutes, or until most of the water has evaporated. Remove the lid and shake the pan to dislodge the dumplings. Cook uncovered for another minute, or until the bottoms of the dumplings are crispy and golden brown. Remove from the pan and repeat to cook the remaining dumplings.

Serve hot, with the dipping sauce and your choice of chilli oil.

Peking Duck Dumplings

These are a twist on traditional Peking duck pancakes. All the classic accompaniments feature in the filling – even cucumber!

MAKES 25

25 Basic dumpling wrappers (page 162)

vegetable oil, for pan-frying

hoisin sauce, to serve

FILLING

1 × 250 g (9 oz) duck breast, skin on

1 tbsp vegetable oil

2 garlic cloves, finely chopped

1 tsp minced ginger

1 spring onion (scallion), finely sliced

2 tbsp hoisin sauce

1 tbsp light soy sauce

1 tsp caster (superfine) sugar

1 tsp salt

½ tsp Chinese five-spice

pinch of ground white pepper

60 g (2 oz) cucumber, cut into tiny cubes

MARINADE

2 tbsp Shaoxing rice wine

¼ tsp Chinese five-spice

¼ tsp salt

To make the filling, place the duck breast in a bowl with the marinade ingredients, massaging thoroughly until well coated. Cover and marinate in the fridge overnight.

When ready to cook, remove the duck from the fridge and bring to room temperature. Preheat the oven to 180°C (350°F).

Place the duck breast, skin side down, in a cast-iron or heavy-based ovenproof frying pan. Over medium–low heat, sear the duck for about 8–10 minutes, until the skin is golden brown and most of the fat has rendered. Flip the breast over and cook for another 2 minutes.

Transfer the pan to the oven and cook for another 5 minutes. Remove from the oven and rest until the meat returns to room temperature. Leaving the skin on, cut the duck breast into tiny pieces and set aside.

Heat the vegetable oil in a frying pan over medium heat. Saute the garlic and ginger for about 30 seconds, until fragrant. Add the duck meat and remaining ingredients, except the cucumber. Stir-fry for 2–3 minutes, until most of the liquid has evaporated. Transfer to a bowl to cool completely. Add the cucumber and stir to mix well.

Fill and shape the dumplings using the gyoza folding technique on page 177.

Heat about 1 tablespoon of oil in a non-stick frying pan over medium heat. Place as many dumplings in the pan as will fit in a single layer without touching each other. Cook for about 2 minutes, until the bottoms of the dumplings turn slightly brown. Pour 60 ml (¼ cup) water into the pan, cover with a lid and increase the heat to medium–high. Steam the dumplings for 3 minutes, or until most of the water has evaporated. Remove the lid and shake the pan to dislodge the dumplings. Cook uncovered for another minute, until the bottoms of the dumplings are crispy and golden brown. Remove from the pan and repeat to cook the remaining dumplings.

Serve hot, with hoisin sauce.

KIMCHI & PORK MANDU

China has jiaozi, Japan has gyoza and Korea has mandu. Originally reserved for royal feasts and festive celebrations, these delightful dumplings have been a staple of the Korean diet for more than 2,000 years. The addition of kimchi introduces a spicy, tangy crunch that contrasts with the savoury pork filling.

MAKES 25

- 25 Basic dumpling wrappers (page 162)
- vegetable oil, for pan-frying
- sesame oil, for drizzling
- Yangnyeom jang (page 171), to serve
- pickled radish, pickled turnip, kimchi, to serve

FILLING

- 25 g (1 oz) dangmyeon (Korean sweet potato glass noodles, see note)
- 120 g (4½ oz) bean sprouts
- 160 g (5½ oz) kimchi, finely chopped
- 100 g (3½ oz) minced (ground) pork, 30% fat
- 100 g (3½ oz) firm tofu, torn and broken into small crumbs
- 2 spring onions (scallions), finely sliced
- 2 garlic cloves, minced
- 1 tsp minced ginger
- 2 tsp sesame oil
- 2 tsp soy sauce
- 2 tsp gochugaru (Korean chilli flakes)
- ¼ tsp salt
- ¼ tsp ground white pepper

To make the filling, add the dangmyeon noodles to a saucepan of boiling water and cook over medium–high heat for 5–6 minutes, until translucent and soft. Drain and finely chop, then transfer to a large bowl.

Blanch the bean sprouts in boiling water for 1 minute. Drain and finely chop, then squeeze out the excess water. Add the bean sprouts to the noodles with the remaining filling ingredients. Using your hand, mix together well.

Fill and shape the dumplings using the gyoza folding technique on page 177.

Heat about 1 tablespoon of vegetable oil in a non-stick frying pan over medium heat. Place as many dumplings in the pan as will fit in a single layer without touching each other. Cook for about 2 minutes, until the bottoms of the dumplings turn slightly brown. Pour 60 ml (¼ cup) water into the pan, cover with a lid and increase the heat to medium–high. Steam the dumplings for 3 minutes, or until most of the water has evaporated. Remove the lid. Drizzle 1 teaspoon of sesame oil into the pan and shake the pan to dislodge the dumplings. Cook uncovered for another minute, until the bottoms of the dumplings are crispy and golden brown. Remove from the pan and repeat to cook the remaining dumplings.

Serve hot, with the dipping sauce, pickled radish, pickled turnip and kimchi.

NOTE: Dangmyeon is a type of glass noodle made with sweet potato starch. You'll find these noodles in any Asian supermarket.

PAN-FRIED PAPER VEGGIE DUMPLINGS

These rice paper dumplings are an easy way to quickly sate your dumpling cravings without the need to make your own dough – or even open a packet of dumpling wrappers! The filling is vegan (just sub out the nuoc cham for another dipping sauce to serve with them). And as rice paper is naturally gluten-free, these are a delicious way to feed pretty much anyone.

MAKES 12

12 rice paper sheets

vegetable oil, for brushing and pan-frying

Nuoc cham (page 167), to serve

FILLING

200 g (7 oz) cabbage, shredded

1 tsp salt

2 tbsp vegetable oil

3 garlic cloves, minced

180 g (6½ oz) firm tofu, torn into crumbs

200 g (7 oz) fresh shiitake mushrooms, finely diced

100 g (3½ oz) shredded carrot

2 tbsp light soy sauce

2 tsp sesame oil

1 tsp salt

1 tsp ground white pepper

2 spring onions (scallions), finely sliced

To make the filling, toss the cabbage and salt together in a bowl and mix well. Leave to sweat for 10 minutes, then squeeze as much liquid out of the cabbage as possible. Discard the liquid and set the cabbage aside.

Heat the vegetable oil in a frying pan over medium–high heat. Saute the garlic for about 30 seconds, until fragrant. Add the tofu and mushrooms and stir-fry for 1 minute, until slightly browned. Toss in the carrot and cabbage and stir-fry for about 3 minutes, until softened. Add the soy sauce, sesame oil, salt and pepper and stir-fry for a minute, or until most of the liquid has evaporated. Turn off the heat. Stir the spring onion through, mixing well. Set aside to cool completely.

Prepare a dumpling wrapping station: set out a shallow bowl or tray of water, a large plate, and a tray brushed with oil.

Dip a rice paper sheet in the water for a few seconds, then place it on the plate and leave for 30 seconds to soften. Place a heaped tablespoon of filling in the centre, then gently lift the sheet from the edge closest to you over the filling. Fold the left and right sides inwards to make an envelope, then roll up tightly to form a rectangular dumpling. Place the dumpling on the oiled tray and repeat with the remaining wrappers and filling.

Heat 2 tablespoons of oil in a frying pan over medium heat. Working in batches, fry the dumplings for 4–5 minutes on each side, until crispy and golden.

Serve hot, with nuoc cham.

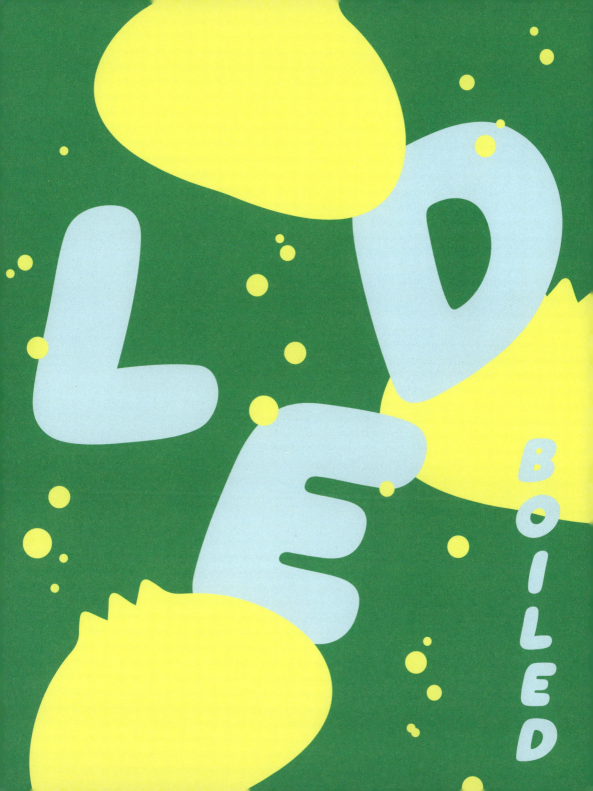

ZUCCHINI & EGG JIAOZI

Zucchini and egg is a common dumpling filling in China during the summer months, as both egg and zucchini are seen to be a light and refreshing ingredients. These dumplings are also vegetarian, making them a popular choice around Lunar New Year.

MAKES 25

25 Basic dumpling wrappers (page 162)

FILLING

15 g (½ oz) small dried shrimp

300 g (10½ oz) zucchini (courgette), grated

1 tsp salt

60 ml (¼ cup) vegetable oil

3 eggs, beaten

2 spring onions (scallions), finely sliced

1 tbsp oyster sauce

1 tsp chicken stock powder

1 tsp ground white pepper

2 tsp sesame oil

To make the filling, soak the dried shrimp in hot water for 1 hour. Drain and set aside. Meanwhile, put the zucchini and salt in a large bowl and massage well. Set aside to sweat for 10 minutes.

Heat 1 tablespoon of the vegetable oil in a frying pan over medium heat. Add the eggs and cook for 5 seconds, then stir the eggs occasionally for about 2 minutes, until the eggs are scrambled into small pieces and fully cooked. Remove from the heat and set aside to cool completely.

Squeeze the zucchini to remove as much liquid as possible, then discard the liquid and transfer the zucchini to a large bowl. Stir the spring onion through, mixing well.

Heat the remaining oil in a saucepan until smoking hot. Carefully pour the hot oil over the zucchini mixture and stir to mix well. Add the scrambled eggs and the remaining filling ingredients, gently stirring everything together until well combined.

Fill and shape the dumplings using the pinching technique on page 174.

Bring a large saucepan of water to a rolling boil over high heat. Working in batches, add the dumplings to the pan, stirring occasionally to stop them sticking together. When the dumplings start to float to the surface and the water boils again, add 60 ml (¼ cup) cold tap water. Repeat this process once or twice for about 8 minutes, until the dumplings are fully cooked.

Remove the dumplings with a wire strainer and transfer to a serving plate. Serve hot, with a dipping sauce of your choice.

VEGAN MUSHROOM & CABBAGE DUMPLINGS

Eating meat is seen to be a cultural marker of prosperity and wealth in China, but veganism has been practised there as far back as the Tang dynasty, when Buddhism was introduced. These substantial dumplings are packed full of mushrooms, cabbage, tofu, carrot and vermicelli noodles.

MAKES 20

20 Basic dumpling wrappers (page 162)

1 spring onion (scallion), green part only, finely sliced, to garnish

Sichuan red chilli oil (page 166), to serve

FILLING

2–3 dried wood ear mushrooms

100 g (3½ oz) cabbage, shredded

1 tsp salt

40 g (1½ oz) glass vermicelli noodles

2 tbsp vegetable oil

3–4 garlic cloves, finely chopped

100 g (3½ oz) firm tofu, finely diced

6 fresh shiitake mushrooms, finely diced

100 g (3½ oz) carrot, shredded

1 bunch coriander (cilantro), finely chopped

1 tbsp light soy sauce

½ tsp salt

1 tsp ground white pepper

1 tbsp cornflour (corn starch), mixed with 60 ml (¼ cup) water

1 tbsp sesame oil

To make the filling, first soak the wood ear mushrooms in hot water for 1 hour to rehydrate. Rinse, trim off the woody parts, then slice the flesh into thin strips and set aside. Meanwhile, toss the cabbage and salt together in a bowl, mixing well. Leave to sweat for 15 minutes, then squeeze as much liquid out of the cabbage as possible. Set aside the cabbage and discard the liquid.

Boil the glass noodles in a saucepan of water over medium–high heat for 5–6 minutes, until cooked. Drain and rinse under cold running water, then finely chop the noodles into tiny pieces. Set aside.

Heat the vegetable oil in a frying pan over medium–high heat and stir-fry the tofu for 1–2 minutes, until slightly brown. Add the cabbage, shiitake and wood ear mushrooms and carrot. Stir-fry for about 3 minutes, until softened. Add the noodles, coriander, soy sauce, salt and pepper and stir-fry for another minute. Give the cornflour slurry a quick stir, pour into the pan and stir for 1 minute, until most of the liquid has evaporated. Turn off the heat and stir in the sesame oil, mixing well. Transfer to a bowl to cool completely.

Fill and shape the dumplings using the pinching technique on page 174.

Bring a large saucepan of water to a rolling boil over high heat. Working in batches, add the dumplings to the pan, stirring occasionally to stop them sticking together. When the dumplings start to float to the surface and the water boils again, add 60 ml (¼ cup) cold tap water. Repeat this process once or twice for about 8 minutes, until the dumplings are fully cooked.

Remove the dumplings with a wire strainer and transfer to a serving plate. Serve hot, topped with the spring onion and a chilli oil or dipping sauce of your choice.

Spicy Pumpkin & Tofu Dumplings

Japanese pumpkin brings a lovely orange colour to these dumplings and pairs perfectly with the warming spices in the filling.

MAKES ABOUT 40

PUMPKIN DOUGH

200 g (7 oz) Japanese pumpkin (winter squash), flesh only

1 egg

1 tbsp cornflour (corn starch)

1 tsp salt

300 g (10½ oz) plain (all-purpose) flour

FILLING

2 tbsp vegetable oil

1 large onion, finely chopped

6 fresh shiitake mushrooms, finely diced

300 g (10½ oz) Japanese pumpkin, peeled and deseeded, finely diced

200 g (7 oz) firm tofu, finely diced

2.5 cm (1 in) piece of ginger, minced

3 red bird's eye chillies, finely chopped

1 tbsp light soy sauce

2 tsp ground coriander

1 tsp each ground turmeric, ground cumin, ground white pepper, and salt

1 tbsp cornflour (corn starch), mixed with 60 ml (¼ cup) water

1 tbsp sesame oil

2 spring onions (scallions), greens only, finely sliced

To prepare the pumpkin dough, finely slice the pumpkin, then place it in a bamboo steamer basket. Cover and steam over a wok of hot simmering water over high heat for about 5 minutes, until soft. Transfer the cooked pumpkin to a saucepan and stir the pumpkin into a mash over medium heat. Cook for 2–3 minutes, until most of the liquid has evaporated.

Scoop the pumpkin mash into a large bowl. Add the egg, cornflour and salt and stir to combine. Stir in half the flour, mixing well. Add the remaining flour and knead in the bowl for 4–5 minutes, until you have a smooth dough. Cover and leave to rest for 20 minutes.

Meanwhile, make the filling. Heat the vegetable oil in a frying pan over medium–high heat. Saute the onion for about 1 minute, until soft and translucent. Add the mushroom and stir-fry for 30 seconds, then add the pumpkin and tofu and stir-fry for 1 minute, or until lightly browned. Add the ginger, chilli, soy sauce, spices and salt and mix well for 20 seconds. Give the cornflour slurry a quick stir and pour into the pan, stirring for about 1 minute, until most of the liquid has evaporated. Turn off the heat and stir in the sesame oil and spring onion, mixing well. Set aside to cool completely.

Roll the pumpkin dough into a log, then cut in half. Roll each log into a long rope about 2.5 cm (1 in) thick, then cut the dough into small individual pieces, weighing about 15 g (½ oz) each.

Fill and shape the dumplings using the pinching technique on page 174.

Bring a large saucepan of water to a rolling boil over high heat. Working in batches, add the dumplings to the pan, stirring occasionally to stop them sticking together. When the dumplings start to float to the surface and the water boils again, add 60 ml (¼ cup) cold tap water. Repeat this process once or twice for about 8 minutes, until the dumplings are fully cooked.

Remove the dumplings with a wire strainer and transfer to a serving plate. Serve hot, with a dipping sauce of your choice.

CHICKEN & WOMBOK JADE DUMPLINGS

These adorable dumplings taste just as good as they look. You can use this two-tone technique with any of your favourite fillings.

MAKES 40–50

SPINACH DOUGH

100 g (3½ oz) spinach, blanched and drained

3–4 ice cubes

2 tbsp water

250 g (9 oz) plain (all-purpose) flour

¼ tsp salt

WHITE DOUGH

250 g (9 oz) plain (all-purpose) flour

¼ tsp salt

100 ml (3½ fl oz) water

FILLING

3–4 dried shiitake mushrooms, soaked in hot water for 1 hour

200 g (7 oz) wombok (Chinese cabbage)

1 tsp salt

2 tbsp white vinegar

400 g (14 oz) minced (ground) chicken

1 tsp minced ginger

3–4 garlic cloves, finely chopped

2 tbsp light soy sauce

2 tsp dark soy sauce

1 tbsp sesame oil

2 tsp oyster sauce

½ tsp ground white pepper

2 spring onions (scallions), finely chopped

To prepare the spinach dough, add the blanched spinach, ice cubes and water to a food processor and blend into a puree. Place 120 g (4½ oz) of the spinach puree in a bowl with the flour and salt and knead to form a rough dough, wrap with plastic wrap and leave to rest for 10 minutes. (While it is resting, you can prepare the white dough.) Knead the dough for 1 minute, then rest for another 10 minutes. Repeat once more until the dough is smooth. Cover and rest for 1 hour.

To prepare the white dough, place the flour, salt and water in another bowl and knead to form a rough dough. Wrap with plastic wrap and follow the resting and kneading instructions as above.

While the doughs are resting, prepare the filling. Finely chop the shiitake mushrooms and reserve 60 ml (¼ cup) of the soaking water. In another bowl, toss the wombok, salt and vinegar together, mixing well. Leave to sweat for 10 minutes, then squeeze as much liquid out of the wombok as possible. Set aside.

In another bowl, combine the chicken, ginger, garlic, soy sauces, sesame oil, oyster sauce and pepper. Stir vigorously until the mixture becomes pasty. Add the wombok and add to the mixture with the spring onion and shiitake mushrooms. Mix well and set aside.

Roll both the white and spinach doughs into a log about 2.5 cm (1 in) thick, ensuring they are the same length. Use a rolling pin to roll the spinach log out into a thin flat sheet about 2 mm (⅟₁₆ in) thick. Spray some water over the surface. Place the white dough log along the edge of the green sheet. Roll the green dough tightly around the white dough, making sure there are no air pockets, until the white dough is fully sealed within. Roll the combined dough into a 2.5 cm (1 in) thick log again, then cut it into 5 mm (¼ in) thick slices. Roll each disc into a thin wrapper, about 11 cm (4¼ in) in diameter.

Fill and shape the dumplings using the pinching technique on page 174.

Boil the dumplings in batches following the boiling instructions on page 95. Remove the dumplings with a wire strainer and transfer to a serving plate. Serve hot, with a dipping sauce of your choice.

BOILED

CHICKEN & SHIITAKE DUMPLINGS

Shiitake mushrooms are native to East Asia, but they are now grown all over the world and are loved for the subtle fragrance and delicate earthiness they bring to whatever they are added to.

MAKES 30

30 Basic dumpling wrappers (page 162)

FILLING

250 g (9 oz) minced (ground) chicken

1 tbsp Shaoxing rice wine

1 tbsp light soy sauce

1 tsp oyster sauce

1 tsp salt

½ tsp ground white pepper

½ tsp caster (superfine) sugar

5–6 fresh shiitake mushrooms, finely diced

50 g (1¾ oz) carrot, finely diced

100 g (½ cup) tinned corn kernels

2 spring onions (scallions), finely sliced

2 tbsp cornflour (corn starch)

1 tbsp sesame oil

To make the filling, place the chicken, rice wine, soy sauce, oyster sauce, salt, pepper and sugar in a bowl and mix until well combined. Stir in the mushrooms, carrot, corn and spring onion, mixing well. Add the cornflour and stir vigorously for about 1 minute, until the mixture is sticky but not wet. Drizzle with the sesame oil and give a quick stir, then cover and refrigerate for 1 hour.

Fill and shape the dumplings using the 'gold ingot' technique on page 176.

Bring a large saucepan of water to a rolling boil over high heat. Working in batches, add the dumplings to the pan, stirring occasionally to stop them sticking together. When the dumplings start to float to the surface and the water boils again, add 60 ml (¼ cup) cold tap water. Repeat this process once or twice for about 8 minutes, until the dumplings are fully cooked.

Remove the dumplings with a wire strainer and transfer to a serving plate. Serve hot, with a dipping sauce of your choice.

No Chinese banquet is complete without a whole fish centrepiece, typically steamed with ginger and spring onions, then drizzled with soy sauce and sesame oil. These fish jiaozi contain those same classic flavours, and feature Spanish mackerel which is a specialty filling from eastern China's coastal province of Shandong. You can substitute the mackerel with another mild white fish for a different, but equally delicious, dumpling.

BAIYU JIAOZI

MAKES 30

30 Basic dumpling wrappers (page 162)

GINGER AND SPRING ONION WATER

2 spring onions (scallions), white part only, finely sliced

2.5 cm (1 in) piece of ginger, julienned

1 tbsp Sichuan peppercorns

250 ml (1 cup) boiling water

FILLING

500 g (1 lb 2 oz) Spanish mackerel fillets, skin off (see note)

15 g (½ oz) pork lard

2 egg whites, lightly beaten

30 g (1 oz) garlic chives, finely sliced

2 tbsp Shaoxing rice wine

1 tbsp sesame oil

1 tbsp salt

1 tbsp ground white pepper

Combine the ginger and spring onion water ingredients in a bowl and leave to infuse for 15 minutes. Pour the liquid through a sieve into a jug, discarding the solids.

To make the filling, cut the fish fillets into smaller pieces. Use a meat cleaver to chop the fish systematically, working from one side to the other. Flip and fold the chopped flesh, and continue to chop in different directions until the mixture resembles a rough fish paste.

Place the fish paste in a large bowl. Add the lard and egg white. Using chopsticks, stir to incorporate. A little bit at a time, add the ginger and spring onion water, stirring until fully absorbed before adding more; the mixture should resemble a wet paste. Add the garlic chives, rice wine, sesame oil, salt and pepper. Keep stirring for 3–5 minutes, until the mixture resembles a thick paste. Cover and set aside to rest for at least 10 minutes, or in the fridge for several hours.

Fill and shape the dumplings using the gyoza folding technique on page 177, or the pinching technique on page 174.

Bring a large saucepan of water to a rolling boil over high heat. Working in batches, add the dumplings to the pan, stirring occasionally to stop them sticking together. When the dumplings start to float to the surface and the water boils again, add 60 ml (¼ cup) cold tap water. Repeat this process once or twice for about 8 minutes, until the dumplings are fully cooked.

Remove the dumplings with a wire strainer and transfer to a serving plate. Serve hot, with a dipping sauce of your choice.

NOTE: If Spanish mackerel isn't available, you can use sea bass or basa.

PRAWN & CHIVE DUMPLINGS

Garlic chives are commonly used across East Asia, both as ornamental plants and as an aromatic herb in cooking. They have a similar flavour and use to regular chives or spring onions (scallions), which makes them a perfect pairing with a variety of meats and seafoods, including prawns. This recipe is a celebration of this classic flavour combination.

MAKES 30

30 Basic dumpling wrappers (page 162)

FILLING

400 g (14 oz) raw prawns (shrimp), peeled and deveined

1 tbsp Shaoxing rice wine

1 tsp salt

1 tsp ground white pepper

2 tbsp cornflour (corn starch)

60 g (2 oz) garlic chives, finely sliced

1 tbsp sesame oil

15 g (½ oz) lard

To make the filling, cut half the prawns into bite-sized pieces and place in a large bowl.

Place one of the remaining prawns on a chopping board and, using the side of a cleaver, smash and smear the meat into paste. One at a time, repeat with the remaining prawns. Gather up all the prawn meat and chop into a fine paste.

Add the prawn paste to the bowl of chopped prawns. Using your hand, stir and massage the mixture for about a minute, until slightly sticky. Add the rice wine, salt and pepper, mixing well. Stir in the cornflour until the mixture is sticky. Stir the garlic chives and sesame oil through until well mixed. Massage in the lard until fully incorporated. Set aside to rest for at least 30 minutes, or no longer than 6 hours in the fridge.

Fill and shape the dumplings using the gyoza folding technique on page 177.

Bring a large saucepan of water to a rolling boil over high heat. Working in batches, add the dumplings to the pan, stirring occasionally to stop them sticking together. When the dumplings start to float to the surface and the water boils again, add 60 ml (¼ cup) cold tap water. Repeat this process once or twice for about 8 minutes, until the dumplings are fully cooked.

Remove the dumplings with a wire strainer and transfer to a serving plate. Serve hot, with a dipping sauce of your choice.

RED CHILLI OIL PORK DUMPLINGS

Sichuan cuisine is known for its love of chilli and its signature mala flavour (meaning 'numbing hot'), which combines the numbing properties of Sichuan peppercorns (ma) with the heat from dried chillis (la). Once you get a taste for it, you'll be hooked for life.

MAKES 30

30 Wonton wrappers (page 163)

sliced spring onion (scallion), to garnish

FILLING

400 g (14 oz) minced (ground) pork, 30% fat

2 tsp salt

2 tsp minced ginger

1 tbsp light soy sauce

1 tbsp oyster sauce

2 tsp sesame oil

½ tsp ground Sichuan peppercorns

½ tsp ground white pepper

1 egg white

80 ml (⅓ cup) water

2 spring onions (scallions), finely sliced

CHILLI OIL DRESSING

3 tbsp Sichuan red chilli oil (page 166)

1 tbsp light soy sauce

1 tsp each white sesame seeds, pork lard, salt, and ground Sichuan peppercorns

½ tsp each ground white pepper and chicken stock powder

To make the filling, place the pork and salt in a bowl. Using chopsticks or your hand, stir the mixture vigorously in one direction for about 3 minutes, until the mixture is pasty. Add the ginger, soy sauce, oyster sauce, sesame oil, Sichuan pepper, white pepper and egg white. Stir until well combined.

Stir in the water a little bit at a time, mixing until all the water is fully absorbed. Add the spring onion and stir vigorously until the mixture is thick and pasty. Cover and refrigerate for 1 hour.

Fill and shape the dumplings using the 'gold ingot' folding technique on page 176.

Combine all the chilli oil dressing ingredients in a large serving bowl, stirring to mix well. Set aside.

Bring a large saucepan of water to a rolling boil over high heat. Working in batches, add the dumplings to the pan, stirring occasionally to stop them sticking together. When the dumplings start to float to the surface and the water boils again, add 60 ml (¼ cup) cold tap water. Repeat this process once or twice for about 8 minutes, until the dumplings are fully cooked.

Add around 125 ml (1/2 cup) of the hot cooking water to the chilli oil dressing, stirring to mix well. Use a wire strainer to transfer the cooked dumplings to the chilli oil dressing. Garnish with sliced spring onions and serve hot.

Simple doesn't have to mean boring. Pork and prawn is a very popular combination across many Chinese cuisines and dishes, and here the classic pairing fills a simple boiled jiaozi (dumpling). Served with your choice of chilli oil or dipping sauce, it's sure to be a favourite.

PORK & PRAWN JIAOZI

MAKES 25

25 Basic dumpling wrappers (page 162)

GINGER AND SPRING ONION WATER

2 spring onions (scallions), white part only, finely sliced

2.5 cm (1 in) piece of ginger, julienned

1 tbsp Sichuan peppercorns

125 ml (½ cup) boiling water

FILLING

250 g (9 oz) minced (ground) pork, 30% fat

1 tbsp oyster sauce

1 tsp salt

1 tsp white sugar

1 tsp chicken stock powder

pinch of ground white pepper

15 g (½ oz) lard

150 g (5½ oz) raw prawn (shrimp) meat, roughly chopped

Combine the ginger and spring onion water ingredients in a bowl and leave to infuse for 15 minutes. Pour the liquid through a sieve into a jug, discarding the solids.

To make the filling, place the pork, oyster sauce, salt, sugar, stock powder and pepper in a large bowl, mixing well. Add half the ginger and spring onion water and stir until fully absorbed, then add the rest and stir vigorously until the mixture is sticky and pasty. Massage the lard through until fully incorporated. Stir in the prawn meat until combined.

Fill and shape the dumplings using the pinching technique on page 174.

Bring a large saucepan of water to a rolling boil over high heat. Working in batches, add the dumplings to the pan, stirring occasionally to stop them sticking together. When the dumplings start to float to the surface and the water boils again, add 60 ml (¼ cup) cold tap water. Repeat this process once or twice for about 8 minutes, until the dumplings are fully cooked.

Remove the dumplings with a wire strainer and transfer to a serving plate. Serve hot, with a chilli oil or dipping sauce of your choice.

PORK & CORIANDER JIAOZI

Jiaozi are one of the most common types of Chinese dumplings. They are generally crescent shaped, made with a wheat-based dough and filled with a combination of pork, spring onions and other herbs, here we've used coriander.

MAKES 30

30 Basic dumpling wrappers (page 162)

FILLING

500 g (1 lb 2 oz) minced (ground) pork, 30% fat

1 tsp salt

2 tbsp light soy sauce

1 tbsp Shaoxing rice wine

1 tbsp sesame oil

1 tbsp white sugar

1 tsp ground white pepper

150 g (5½ oz) coriander (cilantro) leaves, chopped

30 g (1 oz) spring onions (scallions), finely sliced

20 g (¾ oz) minced ginger

To make the filling, place the pork and salt in a large bowl. Using your hand, stir and massage the mixture vigorously for a few minutes, until it is pasty, occasionally scooping up the mixture with your hand and slapping it against the bowl, to help tenderise the meat.

Add the soy sauce, rice wine, sesame oil, sugar and pepper, stirring to mix well. Add the coriander, spring onion and ginger and mix until well combined. Cover and refrigerate for 1 hour.

Fill and shape the dumplings using the pinching technique on page 174.

Bring a large saucepan of water to a rolling boil over high heat. Working in batches, add the dumplings to the pan, stirring occasionally to stop them sticking together. When the dumplings start to float to the surface and the water boils again, add 60 ml (¼ cup) cold tap water. Repeat this process once or twice for about 8 minutes, until the dumplings are fully cooked.

Remove the dumplings with a wire strainer and transfer to a serving plate. Serve hot, with a dipping sauce of your choice.

BEEF & CELERY DUMPLINGS

Beef dumplings reign supreme in northern China, especially in regions with a high proportion of Muslims, namely the Xinjiang region, where both beef and celery are commonly consumed. The root vegetable adds a satisfying crunch to the tender beef filling, with hints of Sichuan pepper lurking in the background.

MAKES 30

30 Basic dumpling wrappers (page 162)

GINGER AND SPRING ONION WATER

2 spring onions (scallions), white part only, finely sliced

2.5 cm (1 in) piece of ginger, julienned

1 tbsp Sichuan peppercorns

250 ml (1 cup) boiling water

FILLING

250 g (9 oz) minced (ground) beef

1 tbsp light soy sauce

1 tsp oyster sauce

1 tsp Shaoxing rice wine

1 tsp minced ginger

1 tsp salt

½ tsp caster (superfine) sugar

½ tsp ground white pepper

1 egg

½ red onion, finely diced

100 g (3½ oz) celery, diced

1 tbsp cornflour (corn starch)

2 tsp sesame oil

Combine the ginger and spring onion water ingredients in a bowl and leave to infuse for 15 minutes. Pour the liquid through a sieve into a jug, discarding the solids.

To make the filling, place the beef, soy sauce, oyster sauce, rice wine, ginger, salt, sugar and pepper in a large bowl. Stir vigorously for about 2 minutes, until well combined and slightly sticky. Mix the egg through. Add half the ginger and spring onion water and stir vigorously until fully absorbed, then add the rest and continue to stir until the mixture is moist but not wet. Mix the red onion and celery through. Add the cornflour and stir for about 1 minute, until the mixture is sticky and pasty. Stir in the sesame oil, mixing well.

Fill and shape the dumplings using the pinching technique on page 174.

Bring a large saucepan of water to a rolling boil over high heat. Working in batches, add the dumplings to the pan, stirring occasionally to stop them sticking together. When the dumplings start to float to the surface and the water boils again, add 60 ml (¼ cup) cold tap water. Repeat this process once or twice for about 8 minutes, until the dumplings are fully cooked.

Remove the dumplings with a wire strainer and transfer to a serving plate. Serve hot, with a dipping sauce of your choice.

BANH BOT LOC

You know banh mi, you've likely tried banh xeo, but have you heard about banh bot loc? These chewy tapioca dumplings hail from the Hue region in central Vietnam, where families come together to prepare them for special occasions, such as the Lunar New Year (Tet). You'll find it hard to stop at just one.

SERVES 4

1 tsp salt

1 tbsp vegetable oil

SPRING ONION OIL

3 spring onions (scallions), green part only, finely sliced

½ tsp salt

125 ml (½ cup) vegetable oil

DIPPING SAUCE

55 g (¼ cup) caster (superfine) sugar

60 ml (¼ cup) fish sauce

185 ml (¾ cup) water

7–8 red bird's eye chillies, finely chopped

Ingredients continue over page →

To prepare the spring onion oil, put the spring onion in a heatproof bowl with the salt. Heat the oil in a small saucepan over high heat until smoking. Carefully pour the hot oil over the spring onion. Once the oil stops splattering, stir to mix well, then set aside to cool.

To make the dipping sauce, combine the sugar, fish sauce and water in a bowl, stirring to dissolve the sugar. Stir in the chilli and set aside.

To make the filling, heat the oil in a frying pan over medium heat and stir-fry the garlic and shallot for about 30 seconds, until fragrant. Add the pork and stir-fry for 2–3 minutes, until cooked. Add the prawn meat and stir for 30 seconds, or until the prawns are barely just cooked through. Stir in the stock powder, salt and sugar and cook for about 3 minutes, until most of the liquid has evaporated and the pork is slightly browned. Turn off the heat. Stir in the annatto oil and pepper and set aside to cool completely.

To make the dough, place the tapioca starch and salt in a bowl, stirring until there are no lumps. Add the hot water and stir until the mixture is slightly sticky. Turn the dough out onto a lightly floured work surface and knead for about 2 minutes, until the dough is smooth and elastic. Cut the dough into four portions. Working with one portion at a time, and keeping the others covered to stop them drying out, roll the dough into a flat sheet about 1 mm (¹⁄₁₆ in) thick. Cut out dumpling wrappers using a 6 cm (2½ in) cookie cutter. Gather up the excess dough and knead back together to make more wrappers.

FILLING

1 tbsp vegetable oil

2 garlic cloves, minced

1 French shallot, minced

100 g (3½ oz) pork belly, cut into tiny pieces

150 g (5½ oz) raw prawn (shrimp) meat, cut into tiny pieces

½ tsp chicken stock powder

½ tsp salt

½ tsp white sugar

1 tbsp annatto oil (see note)

pinch of ground black pepper

DOUGH

200 g (7 oz) tapioca starch, plus extra for dusting

pinch of salt

250 ml (1 cup) boiling water

Place a tiny piece of pork and prawn on a wrapper, fold it in half and pinch around the edges to seal into a dumpling. Repeat with the remaining dough and filling.

Half-fill a large saucepan with water, add a teaspoon of salt and a tablespoon of vegetable oil and bring to a simmer over medium heat. Working in batches, add the dumplings to the water, stir to stop them sticking together, reduce the heat to medium–low and cook for about 5 minutes. Once the dumplings start to float to the surface, cook for another minute. Check their doneness by lifting one out of the water; if the wrapper is transparent, the dumplings are ready.

Using a wire strainer, transfer the cooked dumplings to a bowl of cold water. Once cooled, fish them out and transfer to a serving dish. Drizzle a tablespoon of the spring onion oil over the dumplings and gently toss until well coated, so they don't stick together.

Serve with the dipping sauce and the remaining spring onion oil.

NOTE: Annatto oil can be found at Asian supermarkets specialising in Vietnamese or Filipino cuisine. If not available, you can omit it or substitute with ½ teaspoon sweet paprika in this recipe.

DUMPLINGS 2. Banh bot loc (page 112) 115

HOKKIEN BAK CHANG

Any fans of sticky rice will adore these umami-packed glutinous rice dumplings, which are a cherished dish among the Hokkien community from the Fujian province in southeastern China. Bak chang are traditionally made during the Dragon Boat (Duanwu) Festival to honour the life of ancient poet and patriot Qu Yuan. You will need to begin this recipe the day before serving.

MAKES 12

24–30 dried bamboo leaves

PORK BELLY

250 g (9 oz) pork belly, cut into 2 cm (¾ in) strips

1 tbsp light soy sauce

1 tsp dark soy sauce

2 tsp oyster sauce

2 tsp caster (superfine) sugar

½ tsp Chinese five-spice

pinch of salt

pinch of ground white pepper

SHALLOT OIL

375 ml (1½ cups) vegetable oil

150 g (5½ oz) red Asian shallots, finely sliced

SHIITAKE MUSHROOMS

6 dried shiitake mushrooms, soaked for 3 hours in cold tap water

1 tbsp shallot oil (from above)

1 tsp white sugar

2 tsp light soy sauce

pinch of Chinese five-spice

Ingredients continue over page →

The day before making, place all the pork belly ingredients in a large bowl. Using your hand, massage the mixture into the pork until evenly coated. Cover and marinate overnight in the fridge.

The next day, prepare the bamboo leaves. Fully submerge the leaves in water and soak for 1 hour. Drain, place the leaves in a large saucepan, then fill with water until the bamboo leaves are fully submerged. Boil the leaves over high heat for 10 minutes to soften them. Drain, rinse and wipe dry. Trim off the hard stems, brush the shiny side of the leaves with vegetable oil and set aside.

To make the shallot oil, heat the vegetable oil in a large wok over medium–high heat and stir-fry the shallot for about 5 minutes, until lightly golden. Drain the shallot oil through a sieve into a heatproof bowl and leave to cool completely. Transfer the fried shallots to a bowl and set aside.

To prepare the mushrooms, squeeze out the excess soaking water, trim off the stems, then cut the mushrooms in half. Heat the shallot oil in the same wok over medium–high heat and stir-fry the mushrooms for 10 seconds. Add the remaining ingredients and stir-fry for another minute, or until most of the liquid has been absorbed. Transfer to a bowl and set aside.

To prepare the chestnuts, soak them in cold tap water for 3 hours. Then drain them, split them open and remove any red stem inside. Heat the shallot oil in the same wok and stir-fry the chestnuts for 10 seconds. Add the remaining ingredients and stir-fry for another minute, or until most of the liquid has been absorbed. Transfer to another bowl and set aside.

To prepare the dried shrimp, heat the shallot oil in the same wok and stir-fry the dried shrimp for about 2 minutes, until fragrant. Remove and set aside.

BOILED

CHESTNUTS

12 dried chestnuts (see note)

1 tbsp shallot oil (from opposite)

1 tsp white sugar

1 tsp light soy sauce

pinch of Chinese five-spice

DRIED SHRIMP

1 tbsp shallot oil (from opposite)

40 g (1½ oz) dried shrimp, rinsed to remove excess salt

GLUTINOUS RICE

125 ml (½ cup) shallot oil (from opposite)

500 g (1 lb 2 oz) glutinous rice, soaked for 1 hour in cold tap water, then drained

1 tsp salt

1 tsp white sugar

1 tsp MSG

2 tbsp light soy sauce

1 tbsp oyster sauce

2 tsp dark soy sauce

Heat another 2 tablespoons of the shallot oil in the same wok and stir-fry the marinated pork belly for 2 minutes. Add 125 ml (½ cup) water and stir to dislodge any caramelised bits at the bottom of the wok. Cover with a lid, reduce the heat to low and simmer for 30 minutes. Remove the lid and keep stirring occasionally until most of the liquid has evaporated. Transfer the pork belly to a bowl and set aside.

To prepare the glutinous rice, clean out the wok. Heat the shallot oil over medium heat and stir-fry the rice until well coated. Add the remaining ingredients and stir-fry for 2–3 minutes, until the rice becomes slightly sticky. Transfer to a bowl and set aside.

Prepare a dumpling folding station with all the cooked ingredients in separate bowls. Using the bamboo leaf folding technique on page 178, place a tablespoon of the rice at the bottom of the bamboo cone and compact it down. Add some mushroom, chestnut, pork belly, dried shrimp and fried shallots, then fill with more rice to the top. Finish folding up the dumpling and tie it securely. Repeat with the remaining bamboo leaves, rice and fillings.

Bring a large saucepan of water to a rolling boil over high heat. Gently lower the dumplings into the water and place a heatproof plate on top of the dumplings to keep them fully submerged during cooking. Reduce the heat to low, then cover and simmer for 1 hour and 45 minutes, adding more water whenever the water level drops. Remove the dumplings with a wire strainer and leave to drain and cool for 10 minutes before serving.

NOTE: Dried chestnuts can be found at Asian supermarkets. If using fresh chestnuts, just steam or boil them until soft.

HAKKA CRYSTAL JADE PORK & LEEK DUMPLINGS

The Hakka are a subgroup of Han Chinese people who have settled across the southern Chinese provinces, generally in remote hilly areas. Their cuisine is based around the vegetables and meats that are locally grown and readily available.

MAKES 25–30

1 tsp salt

1 tbsp vegetable oil

coriander (cilantro) leaves, to garnish

Crispy garlic chilli oil (page 165), to serve

CRYSTAL JADE WRAPPERS

200 g (7 oz) potato starch

pinch of salt

125 ml (½ cup) boiling water

60 ml (¼ cup) room-temperature water

1 tsp vegetable oil

FILLING

1 tbsp vegetable oil

100 g (3½ oz) leek (including the green bit), quartered, then finely sliced

250 g (9 oz) minced (ground) pork, 30% fat

2 tbsp fried shallots

1 tbsp light soy sauce

1 tsp each sesame oil, salt, ground white pepper, and caster (superfine) sugar

1 egg

1 tbsp cornflour (corn starch)

To make the filling, heat the vegetable oil in a frying pan over medium heat and stir-fry the leek for about 2 minutes, until softened. Set aside to cool completely. Place the pork in a bowl with the fried shallots, soy sauce, sesame oil, salt, pepper and sugar and mix to combine. Add the leek, egg and cornflour and stir to mix well. Cover and refrigerate until ready to use.

To make the wrappers, mix the potato starch and salt in a large bowl. Pour the boiling water over the mixture and stir until all the water is fully absorbed. Add the room-temperature water and knead in the bowl to form a dough. If it is still dry, add 1 teaspoon of water at a time and keep kneading until it comes together. Add the oil and knead until the dough is smooth and elastic. Cover and leave to rest for 10 minutes.

Tear off a small piece of dough about the size of a walnut (12 g/½ oz) and roll it into a ball. Flatten it into a disc, then roll the dough out into an 8–9 cm (3¼–3½ in) round. Place a small teaspoon of filling in the centre, then pinch the sides of the wrapper towards the centre at three different points to form a triangular pyramid. Pinch the edges together to seal. Repeat with the remaining dough and filling.

Add the salt and oil to a large saucepan of water and bring to a simmer over medium heat. Working in batches, lower the dumplings into the hot water and gently stir to stop them sticking together. Cook the dumplings for about 2 minutes, until they float to the surface. Stirring occasionally, simmer for a further 2–3 minutes.

Remove the dumplings with a wire strainer and transfer to individual serving plates. Garnish with coriander and serve with the chilli oil.

Vegetarian Dumpling Miso Soup

Miso soup is a Japanese staple that is a traditional part of Japanese meals. It is made with miso paste and dashi, but we have used vegetable stock here to keep things vegetarian.

SERVES 6

1 litre (4 cups) Vegetable stock (page 172)

2.5 cm (1 in) piece of ginger, julienned

100 g (3½ oz) shimeji mushrooms, trimmed

1 tbsp white miso paste

30 Basic dumpling wrappers (page 162)

FILLING

200 g (7 oz) cabbage

1 tsp salt

2 tbsp vegetable oil

200 g (7 oz) firm tofu, finely diced

6 fresh shiitake mushrooms, finely diced

60 g (2 oz) carrot, shredded

1 tsp minced ginger

3 garlic cloves, minced

1 bunch coriander (cilantro), finely chopped

1 spring onion (scallion), finely sliced

1 tbsp light soy sauce

1 tsp each salt and ground white pepper

1 tbsp cornflour (corn starch), mixed with 2 tbsp water

1 tbsp sesame oil

TO SERVE

ground white pepper, sesame oil, spring onion

Pour the stock into a saucepan and bring to the boil over medium heat. Add the ginger, mushrooms and miso paste, stirring to dissolve the miso paste. Simmer for 10 minutes, then taste and adjust the seasoning accordingly. Gently simmer for 20–30 minutes to allow the flavours to infuse, then turn off the heat until ready to assemble.

To make the filling, shred the cabbage and toss it with the salt in a bowl, mixing well. Leave to sweat for 20 minutes, then squeeze as much liquid out of the cabbage as possible. Discard the liquid and set the cabbage aside.

Heat the vegetable oil in a frying pan over medium–high heat and stir-fry the tofu for 1–2 minutes, until slightly brown. Add the cabbage, mushroom and carrot and stir-fry for about 3 minutes, until softened. Add the ginger, garlic, coriander, spring onion, soy sauce, salt and pepper and stir-fry for another minute. Give the cornflour slurry a quick stir, pour into the pan and stir for 1 minute, or until most of the liquid has evaporated. Turn off the heat and stir in the sesame oil, mixing well. Transfer to a bowl to cool completely.

Fill and shape the dumplings using the pinching technique on page 174. Return the broth saucepan to the heat, keeping at a gentle simmer, ready to be used.

Bring a large saucepan of water to a rolling boil over high heat. Working in batches, add the dumplings to the water, stirring occasionally to stop them sticking together. When the dumplings start to float to the surface and the water boils again, add 60 ml (¼ cup) cold tap water. Repeat this process once or twice for about 8 minutes, until the dumplings are fully cooked.

Remove the dumplings with a wire strainer and transfer to individual serving bowls.

Pour the hot broth over the dumplings. Season with white pepper and sesame oil, garnish with sliced spring onion and serve.

Wonton soup is the ultimate comfort food, and these vegetarian mushroom and water chestnut wontons make this a comforting dinner for everyone.

SERVES 4

1 litre (4 cups) Vegetable stock (page 172)

1 tbsp light soy sauce

15 Wonton wrappers (page 163)

30 g (1 oz) enoki mushrooms

FILLING

2–3 dried wood ear mushrooms

5 dried shiitake mushrooms

2 tbsp vegetable oil

2.5 cm (1 in) piece of ginger, minced

3 garlic cloves, minced

150 g (5½ oz) fresh shimeji mushrooms, finely chopped

2 tbsp light soy sauce

1 tsp sesame oil

1 tsp white sugar

½ tsp ground white pepper

100 g (3½ oz) water chestnuts, drained and finely chopped

3 spring onions (scallions), finely sliced

2 tsp cornflour (corn starch)

TO SERVE

ground white pepper, sesame oil, sliced spring onion (scallion)

To make the filling, first soak the dried wood ear and shiitake mushrooms in separate bowls of hot water for 1 hour to rehydrate. Rinse the wood ear mushrooms, trim off the woody parts and slice the flesh into thin strips. Squeeze the excess water from the dried shiitake mushrooms, then finely chop and set both mushrooms aside separately.

Meanwhile, pour the stock into a saucepan and bring to the boil over medium heat. Add the soy sauce and stir to mix well. Taste and adjust the seasoning accordingly. Take off the heat until ready to assemble. Trim the enoki mushrooms and separate them into clumps, then set aside.

Heat the vegetable oil in a frying pan over medium–high heat. Stir-fry the ginger and garlic for about 30 seconds, until fragrant. Add the shimeji and shiitake mushrooms and stir-fry for about a minute, until softened. Add the soy sauce, sesame oil, sugar and pepper and stir-fry for another minute, or until most of the liquid has evaporated. Allow to cool.

Transfer the stir-fried mushroom mixture to a food processor and blend into a paste. Tip the mixture into a bowl. Add the wood ear mushrooms, water chestnuts, spring onion and cornflour and stir until well combined.

Fill and shape the dumplings using the 'gold ingot' folding technique on page 176.

Bring a large saucepan of water to a rolling boil over high heat. Working in batches, add the dumplings to the pan, stirring occasionally to stop them sticking together. When the dumplings start to float to the surface and the water boils again, add 60 ml (¼ cup) cold tap water. Repeat this process once or twice for about 8 minutes, until the dumplings are fully cooked.

Remove the dumplings with a wire strainer and transfer to individual serving bowls.

Five minutes before serving, return the broth to the heat and gently simmer, add the enoki mushrooms and simmer until just cooked. Pour the hot broth over the dumplings. Season with white pepper and sesame oil, garnish with spring onion and serve.

DUMPLINGS

PORK & PRAWN WONTON SOUP

Beautifully folded pork and prawn wontons floating in a fragrant stock, served with bok choy and plenty of pickled green chillies on the side – it really is the perfect dinner.

SERVES 6

- 1 litre (4 cups) Vegetable stock (page 172)
- 1 tbsp light soy sauce
- 1 tsp chicken stock powder
- 30 Wonton wrappers (page 163)
- 3 baby bok choy, halved lengthways

FILLING

- 250 g (9 oz) minced (ground) pork, 30% fat
- 2.5 cm (1 in) piece of ginger, minced
- 2 spring onions (scallions), finely sliced
- 1 tbsp light soy sauce
- 1 tsp each Shaoxing rice wine, sesame oil, and caster (superfine) sugar
- ½ tsp ground white pepper
- ¼ tsp salt
- 250 g (9 oz) raw prawn (shrimp) meat, roughly chopped

TO SERVE

- 1 spring onion (scallion), finely sliced
- 1 bunch coriander (cilantro), leaves picked
- ground white pepper, to taste
- sesame oil, to taste
- Pickled green chillies (page 170)

Pour the stock into a saucepan and bring to the boil over medium heat. Add the soy sauce and stock powder and stir to mix well. Taste and adjust the seasoning accordingly. Gently simmer for 20–30 minutes to allow the flavours to infuse, then turn off the heat until ready to assemble.

To make the filling, place all the ingredients, except the prawn meat, in a large bowl and stir vigorously until well combined. Add 2 tablespoons of the vegetable broth and stir for another minute to form a wet paste. Add the prawn meat and gently stir to combine.

Place a heaped teaspoon of filling in the centre of a wonton wrapper. Dab your finger in water, then run it along the edges of the wrapper. Gather up all the corners towards the middle, then pinch together close to the filling to make sure there are no air pockets and seal firmly. Repeat with the remaining wrappers and filling.

Return the broth saucepan to the heat, keeping at a gentle simmer, ready to be used.

Bring a large saucepan of water to a rolling boil over high heat. Working in batches, add the dumplings to the water, stirring occasionally to stop them sticking together. When the dumplings start to float to the surface and the water boils again, add 60 ml (¼ cup) cold tap water. Repeat this process once or twice for about 8 minutes, until the dumplings are fully cooked.

When the dumplings are very nearly ready, blanch the bok choy in the same pan of water for 30 seconds.

Remove the dumplings with a wire strainer and transfer to individual serving bowls. Top with the bok choy.

Pour the hot broth over the dumplings. Garnish with the spring onion and coriander, then season with white pepper and sesame oil. Serve immediately, with pickled green chillies with soy sauce.

BEEF DUMPLING PHO SOUP

This is a play on a classic Vietnamese pho bo (beef pho), but deliciously plump beef-filled dumplings have replaced the sliced beef and the rice noodles. It's worth taking your time when simmering the Pho stock – the longer it simmers, the deeper the flavour. Your effort will absolutely be rewarded.

SERVES 4–5

1.5 litres (6 cups) Pho stock (page 173)

25 Basic dumpling wrappers (page 162)

GINGER AND SPRING ONION WATER

2 spring onions (scallions), finely sliced

2.5 cm (1 in) piece of ginger, julienned

1 tbsp Sichuan peppercorns

250 ml (1 cup) boiling water

FILLING

250 g (9 oz) minced (ground) beef

½ tsp minced ginger

1 tbsp oyster sauce

1 tbsp light soy sauce

2 tsp dark soy sauce

2 tsp Shaoxing rice wine

1 tsp salt

1 tsp Chinese five-spice

½ tsp ground white pepper

Ingredients continue over page →

Combine the ginger and spring onion water ingredients in a bowl and leave to infuse for 15 minutes. Pour the liquid through a sieve into a jug, discarding the solids.

Meanwhile, pour the stock into a saucepan and bring to the boil over medium heat. Keep at a gentle simmer, ready to be used.

To make the filling, place the beef, ginger, oyster sauce, soy sauces, rice wine, salt, five-spice and pepper in a large bowl. Stir vigorously for about 2 minutes, until the mixture is sticky. Add half the ginger and spring onion water and stir until fully absorbed, then add the rest and stir vigorously until the mixture is sticky and pasty. Add the cornflour and stir until there are no flour lumps. Stir the sesame oil, Thai basil and spring onion through, mixing well.

Fill and shape the dumplings using the pinching technique on page 174.

Bring a large saucepan of water to a rolling boil over high heat. Working in batches, add the dumplings to the pan, stirring occasionally to stop them sticking together. When the dumplings start to float to the surface and the water boils again, add 60 ml (¼ cup) cold tap water. Repeat this process once or twice for about 8 minutes, until the dumplings are fully cooked.

2 tbsp cornflour
(corn starch)

1 tbsp sesame oil

1 bunch Thai basil leaves, finely chopped

2–3 spring onions (scallions), finely sliced

TO SERVE

½ onion, finely sliced

handful of bean sprouts

1 bunch Thai basil, leaves picked

3–4 red bird's eye chillies, finely sliced

2 spring onions (scallions), sliced

4–6 lime wedges

hoisin sauce, for dipping

Dim sum chilli sauce (page 167), for dipping

Remove the dumplings with a wire strainer and transfer to individual serving bowls. Top with the onion and bean sprouts.

Pour the hot broth over the dumplings. Garnish with the Thai basil leaves, chilli, spring onion and a wedge of lime. Serve immediately, with hoisin and chilli sauce on the side.

Beef dumpling pho soup (page 126)

DUMPLINGS 129

CHICKEN & CORN DUMPLING SOUP

Chicken and sweetcorn soup, or egg drop soup, is a beloved Chinese restaurant classic – and it's not hard to see why! Dumplings aren't a traditional addition, but they are a delicious one.

SERVES 4

1 litre (4 cups) Vegetable stock (page 172)

100 g (½ cup) tinned corn kernels

1 tbsp light soy sauce

1 tsp chicken stock powder

1 tbsp cornflour (corn starch), mixed with 2 tbsp water

1 egg, beaten

20 Basic dumpling wrappers (page 162)

FILLING

100 g (3½ oz) wombok (Chinese cabbage), finely chopped

1 tsp salt

250 g (9 oz) minced (ground) chicken

2.5 cm (1 in) piece of ginger, minced

100 g (½ cup) tinned corn kernels

1 tbsp light soy sauce

TO SERVE

ground white pepper, to taste

light soy sauce, to taste

Chinkiang black vinegar, to taste

coriander (cilantro) leaves

To make the filling, toss the cabbage and salt together in a bowl, mixing well. Leave to sweat for 30 minutes, then squeeze as much liquid out of the cabbage as possible. Discard the liquid and add the remaining filling ingredients to the bowl then stir vigorously until well combined. The mixture should be sticky but not overly wet.

Meanwhile, pour the stock into a saucepan, add the corn kernels and bring to the boil over medium heat. Add the soy sauce and stock powder and stir to mix well. Keep at a gentle simmer, ready to be used.

Fill and shape the dumplings using the pinching technique on page 174.

Bring a large saucepan of water to a rolling boil over high heat. Working in batches, add the dumplings to the pan, stirring occasionally to stop them sticking together. When the dumplings start to float to the surface and the water boils again, add 60 ml (¼ cup) cold tap water. Repeat this process once or twice for about 8 minutes, until the dumplings are fully cooked.

Remove the dumplings with a wire strainer and transfer to individual serving bowls.

Just before serving, give the cornflour slurry a quick stir and pour into the broth, mixing well. Keep stirring and slowly pour the beaten egg into the broth to create an egg floss. Taste and adjust the seasoning accordingly. Pour the hot broth over the dumplings. Season with white pepper, soy sauce and black vinegar, garnish with coriander and serve.

Chicken Wonton Laksa Soup

Laksa is a Peranakan Chinese noodle soup that is popular across Southeast Asia, particularly in Malaysia, Singapore and Indonesia. There are many variations, but it is generally served with thick rice noodles and a spicy coconut milk–based curry soup.

SERVES 4

20 Wonton wrappers (page 163)

LAKSA BROTH

2 tbsp vegetable oil

60 g (¼ cup) laksa paste

1 litre (4 cups) chicken stock

400 ml (13½ fl oz) tin coconut milk

1 tbsp fish sauce

100 g (3½ oz) fried tofu puffs, halved

FILLING

100 g (3½ oz) wombok (Chinese cabbage), finely chopped

2 tsp salt

250 g (9 oz) boneless, skinless chicken thighs, cut into small chunks

½ onion, finely chopped

2 garlic cloves, peeled

1 tbsp cornflour (corn starch)

½ tsp ground black pepper

1 spring onion (scallion), finely sliced

TO SERVE

bean sprouts, finely sliced red chilli, coriander (cilantro) leaves, fried shallots

To prepare the laksa broth, heat the vegetable oil in a large saucepan over medium heat and stir-fry the laksa paste for 2–3 minutes, until it smells fragrant and the oil has separated. Stir in the stock, coconut milk and fish sauce, then bring to the boil over medium–high heat. Add the tofu puffs. Taste and adjust the seasoning accordingly. Gently simmer for 20–30 minutes to allow the flavours to infuse, then turn off the heat until ready to assemble.

To make the filling, toss the wombok and 1 teaspoon of the salt together in a bowl, mixing well. Leave to sweat for 30 minutes, then squeeze as much liquid out of the wombok as possible. Discard the liquid and set the wombok aside.

Place the chicken in a food processor with the remaining 1 teaspoon of salt. Add the onion, garlic, cornflour and pepper and blend into a paste. Tip the mixture into a large bowl and add the wombok and spring onion, stir to mix well.

Place a heaped teaspoon of filling in the centre of a wonton wrapper. Dab your finger in water, then run it along the edges of the wrapper. Gather up all the corners towards the middle, then pinch together close to the filling to make sure there are no air pockets and seal firmly. Repeat with the remaining filling and wrappers.

Return the broth saucepan to the heat, keeping at a gentle simmer, ready to be used. Bring a large saucepan of water to a rolling boil over high heat. Working in batches, add the dumplings to the water, stirring occasionally to stop them sticking together. When the dumplings start to float to the surface and the water boils again, add 60 ml (¼ cup) cold tap water. Repeat this process once or twice for about 8 minutes, until the dumplings are fully cooked.

Remove the dumplings with a wire strainer and transfer to individual serving bowls.

Pour the hot laksa broth over the dumplings. Top with the tofu puffs, bean sprouts, chilli, coriander and fried shallots and serve.

PRAWN WONTON TOM YUM SOUP

Tom yum, or tom yam, is a hot and sour Thai soup with a fragrant broth that is loved all over the world.

SERVES 6

30 Wonton wrappers (page 163)

coriander (cilantro) leaves and sliced red chillies, to garnish

TOM YUM BROTH

2 tbsp vegetable oil

prawn heads and shells, reserved from the dumpling filling

1 litre (4 cups) water

4–5 makrut lime leaves

2 lemongrass stems, stems smashed

2.5 cm (1 in) piece of fresh galangal, sliced

2 red bird's eye chillies, smashed

150 g (5½ oz) oyster mushrooms, cut into bite-sized pieces

1 tomato, cut into wedges

2 tbsp fish sauce

2 tsp white sugar

60 ml (¼ cup) lime juice

FILLING

400 g (14 oz) raw prawns (shrimp), shells reserved for the broth

60 g (2 oz) water chestnuts, finely diced

4–5 coriander (cilantro) stems, finely chopped

2 tsp sesame oil

1 tsp each fish sauce, salt, and ground white pepper

To prepare the broth, heat the vegetable oil in a saucepan over medium–high heat and stir-fry the prawn heads and shells for 2 minutes, until they are bright red and release their oil essence. Pour in the water and bring to the boil. Cover, reduce the heat to medium and simmer for 10 minutes.

Pour the prawn stock through a sieve into a large saucepan, discarding the solids. Add the lime leaves, lemongrass, galangal and chillies and simmer over medium heat for 10 minutes. Add the mushrooms and tomato and simmer for 3 minutes. Season with the fish sauce, sugar and lime juice and simmer for another minute. Taste and adjust the seasoning accordingly. Keep the broth at a gentle simmer, ready to be used.

To make the filling, place half the prawns in a blender and blitz into a paste. Chop the remaining prawns into bite-sized pieces and place in a bowl with the prawn paste, mixing well. Add the remaining filling ingredients and stir until well combined. Cover and marinate in the fridge for at least 10 minutes, or for no more than 6 hours.

Place a heaped teaspoon of filling in the centre of a wrapper. Dab your finger in water, then run it along the edges of the wrapper. Gather up all the corners towards the middle, then pinch together close to the filling to make sure there are no air pockets and seal firmly. Repeat with the remaining filling and wrappers.

Bring a large saucepan of water to a rolling boil over high heat. Working in batches, add the dumplings to the pan, stirring occasionally to stop them sticking together. When the dumplings start to float to the surface and the water boils again, add 60 ml (¼ cup) cold tap water. Repeat this process once or twice for about 8 minutes, until the dumplings are fully cooked.

Remove the dumplings with a wire strainer and transfer to individual serving bowls.

Pour the hot tom yum broth over the dumplings, along with some of the mushrooms and tomato. Garnish with coriander and some sliced red chilli and serve.

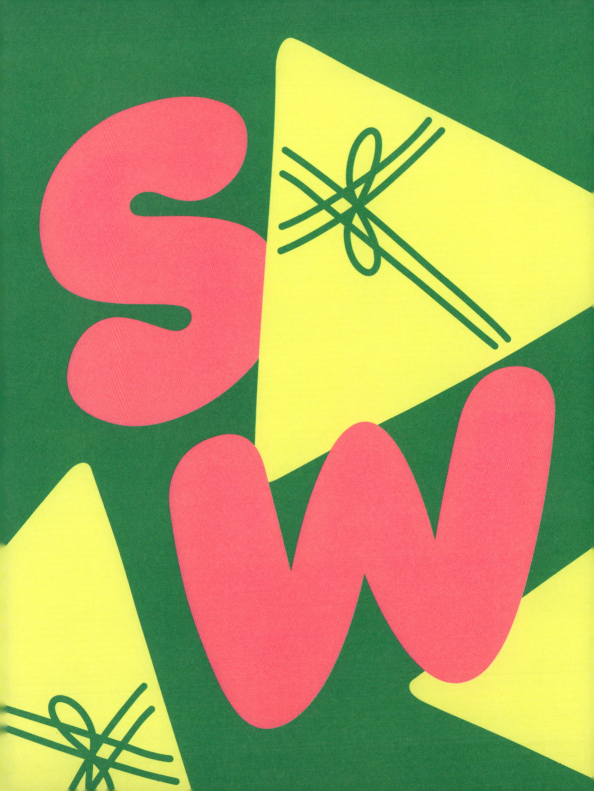

PEANUT TANG YUAN

These sweet, nutty, flavour bombs are a festival staple during the Lantern Festival and Winter Solstice (Dongzhi Festival) in regions of southern China – particularly in Canton and Hakka communities where peanuts are a staple ingredient, as their round shape symbolises family reunions and togetherness. The sticky, glutinous rice skin resembles Japanese mochi in texture, but it's served in a warm, ginger-infused syrup.

MAKES 14

FILLING

150 g (5½ oz) roasted peanuts

50 g (1¾ oz) white sugar

2 tbsp water

60 g (2 oz) unsalted butter, at room temperature

GLUTINOUS RICE DOUGH

250 g (9 oz) glutinous rice flour, plus extra for dusting

180 ml (6 fl oz) boiling water

60 ml (¼ cup) room-temperature water

Ingredients continue over page →

To make the filling, place the peanuts in a food processor and blend into a paste. Scrape down the sides of the blender, then continue to blend until there are no big crumbs.

In a saucepan, bring the sugar and water to the boil over medium–high heat. When the bubbles in the hot sugar syrup start getting bigger and slowing down (the thread stage: 106°C/223°F), turn off the heat. Add the butter and stir until fully melted. Leave to cool to room temperature.

Stir the peanut paste through the sugar mixture, mixing well. Pour the mixture into a zip-lock bag. Seal the bag, then spread the mixture evenly inside, to about a 1 cm (½ in) thickness. Keep the mixture flat and place it in the freezer for about 30 minutes, until semi-firm.

To make the dough, place the rice flour in a heatproof bowl. Pour the hot water over the flour, then stir with a pair of chopsticks until fully absorbed. Add the room-temperature water and stir until the dough slowly comes together. When cool enough to handle, knead the dough for 2–3 minutes, until smooth and elastic. Cover and leave to rest for 20 minutes.

Take the peanut filling out of the freezer and cut the zip-lock bag open. Cut the block into 1.5 cm (½ in) strips, then cut each strip into 1.5 cm (½ in) cubes (about 8 g/¼ oz each). Roll each cube into a ball, then place them on a tray and transfer to the freezer to firm up again while finishing the dough.

Roll the dough out into a log, then cut it into three equal pieces. Working with one piece at a time, and keeping the others wrapped to stop them drying out, roll the dough into a long 2 cm (¾ in) rope and cut the rope into small walnut-sized pieces, weighing about 15 g (½ oz) each.

GINGER BROWN SUGAR SYRUP

1 litre (4 cups) water

25 g (1 oz) old ginger, finely sliced

20 g (¾ oz) dark brown sugar

80 g (2¾ oz) white sugar

2 fresh or frozen (thawed) pandan leaves, tied into a knot

Roll each dough piece into a ball, then press your thumb in the centre to make an indentation and gently stretch it out to form a small cup. Place one cube of the frozen peanut filling inside the dough cup, then slowly wrap the dough up and pinch to seal the edges. Roll the dough into a ball again, then place it on a tray dusted with glutinous rice flour to prevent sticking. Repeat with the remaining dough and filling.

Place all the ginger brown sugar syrup ingredients in a saucepan and bring to a simmer over medium heat, stirring until the sugar has dissolved. Simmer for 10 minutes, then remove the pandan leaves, turn off the heat, cover and keep warm.

Half-fill a saucepan with water and bring to a simmer over medium heat. Working in batches, drop some rice balls into the hot water and gently stir occasionally to stop them sticking together. Once the balls float to the surface, cook for a further minute. Remove with a wire strainer and transfer to a bowl of cold water to cool down.

Place three or four dumplings in each serving bowl, pour ladlefuls of the warm ginger syrup over them and serve warm.

NOTE: Pandan leaves have a sweet aroma and are often used as a vanilla substitute in the cuisines of Southeast Asia. Fresh or frozen pandan leaves are available at Asian supermarkets.

1. Peanut tang yuan (page 138)

DUMPLINGS 2. Black sesame tang yuan (page 142) 141

Black Sesame Tang Yuan

Rich, creamy black sesame paste encased in chewy glutinous rice dough makes for one of the best dessert dumplings around. While peanut tang yuan are particularly popular in southern China, their black sesame sister is believed to have originated in northern regions like Shandong and Beijing. A ladle of sweetened soy milk complements the nutty richness of these tang yuan.

MAKES 14

FILLING

80 g (2¾ oz) black sesame seeds

30 g (1 oz) walnuts

40 g (1½ oz) white sugar

50 g (1¾ oz) unsalted butter, melted

2 tbsp honey

GLUTINOUS RICE DOUGH

250 g (9 oz) glutinous rice flour, plus extra for dusting

180 ml (6 fl oz) boiling water

60 ml (¼ cup) room-temperature water

Ingredients continue over page →

To make the filling, place the black sesame seeds, walnuts and sugar in a food processor and blend into a powder. Transfer to a bowl, add the melted butter and mix well. Stir in the honey until well combined.

Pour the mixture into a zip-lock bag. Seal the bag, then spread the mixture evenly inside, to about a 1 cm (½ in) thickness. Keep the mixture flat and place it in the freezer for about 30 minutes, until semi-firm.

To make the dough, place the rice flour in a heatproof bowl. Pour the hot water over the flour, then stir with a pair of chopsticks until fully absorbed. Add the room-temperature water and stir until the dough slowly comes together. When cool enough to handle, knead the dough for 2–3 minutes, until smooth and elastic. Cover and leave to rest for 20 minutes.

Take the black sesame filling out of the freezer and cut the zip-lock bag open. Cut the block into 1.5 cm (½ in) strips, then cut each strip into 1.5 cm (½ in) cubes (about 8 g/¼ oz each). Roll each cube into a ball, place them on a tray and transfer to the freezer to firm up again while finishing the dough.

Roll the dough out into a log, then cut it into three equal pieces. Working with one piece at a time, and keeping the others wrapped to stop them drying out, roll the dough into a long 2 cm (¾ in) rope and cut it into walnut-sized pieces, weighing about 15 g (½ oz) each.

Roll each piece into a ball, press your thumb in the centre to make an indentation, then gently stretch it out to form a small cup. Place one cube of the frozen filling inside the dough cup, then slowly wrap the dough up and pinch to seal the edges. Roll the dough into a ball again, then place it on a tray dusted with glutinous rice flour to prevent sticking. Repeat with the remaining dough and filling.

SWEET SOY MILK

1 litre (4 cups) soy milk

3–4 fresh or frozen (thawed) pandan leaves, tied into a knot

150 g (5½ oz) caster (superfine) sugar

To make the sweet soy milk, place the soy milk and pandan leaves in a saucepan and bring to a simmer over medium heat. Add the sugar and stir until dissolved, then simmer for 10 minutes. Remove the pandan leaves, turn off the heat, then cover and keep warm.

Half-fill a saucepan with water and bring to a simmer over medium heat. Working in batches, drop some rice balls into the hot water and gently stir occasionally to stop them sticking together. Once the balls float to the surface, cook for a further minute. Remove with a wire strainer and transfer to a bowl of cold water to cool.

Place three or four dumplings in each serving bowl, pour ladlefuls of the warm soy milk over them and serve warm.

Pictured previous

GOK ZAI

Fill, fold, fry, repeat. These peanut pastry puffs, called gok zai or yau gok in Cantonese, are folded into crescent shapes with crimped edges, before being fried to golden perfection. With a fragrant filling of roasted peanuts, coconut and sesame seeds, they're a favourite sweet treat for kids during Lunar New Year celebrations.

MAKES ABOUT 30

vegetable oil, for deep-frying

FILLING

100 g (3½ oz) roasted peanuts

30 g (1 oz) desiccated coconut, toasted

20 g (¾ oz) sesame seeds, toasted

50 g (1¾ oz) caster (superfine) sugar

DOUGH

300 g (10½ oz) plain (all-purpose) flour, sifted

1 egg, beaten

20 g (¾ oz) caster (superfine) sugar

80 g (2¾ oz) lard, melted

50 ml (1¾ fl oz) water

½ tsp salt

To make the filling, place the peanuts in a zip-lock bag and seal the bag, then use a rolling pin to crush the peanuts into crumbs. Alternatively, place the peanuts in a blender and blitz into fine crumbs using the 'pulse' mode. Tip into a bowl, add the coconut, sesame seeds and sugar and mix well.

To prepare the dough, place the flour in a bowl. In another bowl, whisk the egg and sugar together for about 1 minute, until the sugar has dissolved. Add to the flour with the lard and stir until well combined. Add half the water and use your hand to knead everything together. If the mixture is dry, add more water, a tablespoon at a time, and continue to knead into a smooth dough. Wrap in plastic wrap and leave to rest for 30 minutes.

Tip the dough out onto a floured work surface and roll it out into a flat sheet, about 2 mm (¹⁄₁₆ in) thick. Use a 5 cm (2 in) cookie cutter to cut the dough into round wrappers. Gather up the offcuts, roll them back into a dough, rest the dough again and repeat the process to make more wrappers.

Place a teaspoon of filling in the centre of a wrapper. Fold the disc in half, into a half-moon shape, and pinch around the edges to seal. Starting from one end, pinch the edge thinly, fold it inward on an angle and pinch to crimp the edge. Continue this movement to make pleats along the edge. Repeat with the remaining dough and filling.

Half-fill a large saucepan or wok with oil and heat to 155–160°C (310–320°F) over medium–low heat. Test the oil is at the right temperature by dipping a wooden chopstick in it; if the oil bubbles gently, it is ready. Working in batches, fry the dumplings, flipping them continuously, for 8–10 minutes, until golden brown. Remove with a wire strainer and transfer to a tray lined with paper towel to cool completely.

The dumplings are best served fresh, but will keep in an airtight container in the pantry for up to 2 weeks.

SAGO ZONGZI

Loved for its chewy texture, sago zongzi boasts a bouncy, transparent skin similar to that of Jianshui zongzi (page 154). The jelly-like exterior is made from sago tapioca pearls – yes, the same pearls found in bubble tea – and stuffed with a sweet red bean paste.

MAKES 10–15

- 20–30 dried bamboo leaves (see note)
- vegetable oil, for brushing
- 200 g (7 oz) tapioca (sago) pearls
- 50 g (1¾ oz) caster (superfine) sugar
- 2 tbsp vegetable oil, plus extra for brushing
- 160 ml (⅔ cup) water
- 100 g (3½ oz) red bean paste (see note)
- coconut cream, for drizzling (optional)

To prepare the bamboo leaves, fully submerge them in water and soak for 1 hour. Drain, then place the leaves in a large saucepan and fill with water until fully submerged. Boil the leaves over high heat for 10 minutes to soften them. Drain, rinse and wipe dry. Trim off the hard stems, brush the shiny side of the leaves with vegetable oil and set aside.

Put the tapioca pearls in a large bowl, add the sugar and mix well. Add the oil and stir until well coated. Add the water in three batches, stirring and leaving to sit for about 10 minutes after each addition until the water is absorbed by the tapioca.

Fold the bamboo leaves into a cone, following the instructions on page 178. Fill the bottom of the bamboo leaf cone with 2 teaspoons of the tapioca pearls, then 1 teaspoon of the red bean paste. Cover the filling with another 2 teaspoons of tapioca pearls. Continue wrapping the dumpling using the bamboo leaf folding technique on page 178. Repeat with the remaining leaves and filling.

Arrange the dumplings neatly and snugly in a large saucepan. Pour in enough water to come just above the dumplings. Place a heatproof plate on top of the dumplings to weigh them down during cooking. Bring the water to the boil over medium–high heat. Cover, reduce the heat to medium–low and boil for 40 minutes.

Remove the dumplings and leave to cool to room temperature. The dumplings will keep in an airtight container in the fridge for up to 3 days, or in the freezer for up to 3 months.

To serve, peel the leaves off the dumplings, transfer to small plates and drizzle with coconut cream, if desired.

NOTE: Dried bamboo leaves are available at Asian supermarkets. Be sure to prepare and clean the leaves before using.

Instead of using red bean paste, other popular options include sweet mung bean paste or mango.

BUKKUMI

Both chewy and crispy at the same time, these sweet Korean rice cakes are one of the quickest dumplings to prepare. Bukkumi – originating from the Gangwon-do province of Korea – are pan-fried to create a crispy crust that encases a gooey red bean filling. Once sealed, they're garnished with edible flowers and can be drizzled with honey for an extra touch of sweetness.

MAKES 10

vegetable oil, for pan-frying

sesame oil, for pan-frying

130 g (4½ oz) tinned red bean paste (see note)

edible flower petals and leaves (such as marigold, viola, nasturtium), to garnish

honey, to taste (optional)

DOUGH

200 g (7 oz) glutinous rice flour, plus extra for dusting

¼ tsp salt

160 ml (⅔ cup) boiling water

To make the dough, mix the rice flour and salt in a bowl, add the boiling water and stir with a wooden spoon until it all comes together. Taking care as the mixture is still hot, use your hand to knead the mixture into a rough dough. If it's too dry, just add another tablespoon of boiling water and knead again. Wrap the dough in plastic wrap and leave to rest for 10 minutes.

Knead the dough for about 2 minutes, until smooth. Tear off a piece of dough and roll it into a ball about the size of a golf ball. Repeat with the remaining dough, then roll each ball into a 12 cm (4¾ in) round, about 2 mm (1/16 in) thick.

Heat 1 tablespoon of vegetable oil and a drizzle of sesame oil in a non-stick frying pan over medium–low heat, swirling the pan around to coat it evenly. Working in batches, place the dough discs in the pan and fry for about 2 minutes, until a light crust starts to form underneath. Flip the discs over and fry for another 2 minutes, then remove from the pan.

Place a heaped teaspoon of red bean paste, slightly off centre, on a cooked dough disc. Fold the disc in half, into a half-moon shape. Using the back of a wooden spoon, press the edges together to seal. Repeat with the remaining wrappers and red bean paste.

Using the same frying pan, cook the dumplings for about 1 minute, until the bottom is crunchy and light golden brown. You may need to do this in batches. Decorate each dumpling with flower petals, flip them over, flatten with a spatula and cook for another 5 seconds, then transfer the dumplings to a serving plate.

Serve the dumplings warm, with some honey if desired.

NOTE: You can find tinned red bean paste (also called azuki bean paste) in Asian supermarkets. Tinned red bean paste is slightly wet, so you will need to cook it down slightly over low heat until it is slightly dry, like potato mash, to make it easier to roll into a ball.

KRONG KRANG NAM KATI

Shaped like Italian gnocchi and easily mistaken for gummy worms, this beloved Thai dessert showcases two of the country's most popular ingredients – tapioca flour and coconut milk. You can get creative with vibrant food colourings so that the dumplings stand out once they are submerged in the creamy coconut milk soup.

SERVES 4

- 200 g (7 oz) tapioca flour
- 200 ml (7 fl oz) boiling water
- red and green food colouring
- white sesame seeds, toasted, to garnish

COCONUT SYRUP

- 500 ml (2 cups) coconut milk
- 200 ml (7 fl oz) water
- 120 g (4½ oz) caster (superfine) sugar
- ½ tsp salt

Put the tapioca flour in a bowl, pour the boiling water over and stir with a pair of chopsticks to mix it all through. When the mixture is cool enough to handle, knead in the bowl for 1–2 minutes, to form a soft dough.

Divide the dough into three equal portions. Keep one portion as a white dough; add 1–2 drops of red food colouring to the second portion and knead to make a pink dough; add 1 drop of green food colouring to the third portion and knead to make a green dough.

Tear off a small piece of dough (about 3 g/⅛ oz) and roll it into an oval shape. Using your thumb, firmly press the dough onto a gnocchi board or sushi mat, then smear and roll forward to create ridges so it looks like a little cocoon. Repeat with the remaining white, pink and green dough.

Bring a large saucepan of water to a rolling boil over high heat. Add the dumplings, stirring occasionally to stop them sticking to the bottom of the pan. When the water comes back to the boil, reduce the heat to medium and simmer for 5 minutes, or until the dumplings are slightly transparent. Remove with a wire strainer and transfer to a bowl of iced cold water to cool to room temperature.

Place all the coconut syrup ingredients in a saucepan and bring to a simmer over medium–low heat. Stir until the sugar has dissolved, then add all the drained dumplings to the syrup and cook for 2 minutes. Remove from the heat and cool to room temperature.

Serve the dumplings in individual serving bowls, drizzled with the coconut syrup and garnished with sesame seeds.

HANAMI DANGO

Hanami dango is a Japanese confectionery named after the cultural celebration of flower viewing (hanami), which marks the arrival of spring. These chewy rice balls are traditionally served on skewers and come in three distinct colours – pink to symbolise cherry blossoms, white to represent the remaining snow of winter, and green to reflect fresh young grass. Although not strictly traditional, we like adding a drizzle of honey for extra sweetness.

MAKES 8

60 g (2 oz) glutinous rice flour

60 ml (¼ cup) room-temperature water

60 g (2 oz) rice flour

2 tbsp caster (superfine) sugar

60 ml (¼ cup) boiling water

½ tsp matcha powder

red food colouring

honey, to taste (optional)

Combine the glutinous rice flour and room-temperature water in a bowl and mix well.

In a heatproof bowl, combine the rice flour, sugar and boiling water, stirring to form a dough. Add to the glutinous rice flour mixture and knead them together in the bowl for about 2 minutes, until smooth. Divide the dough into three equal portions, then cover with a tea towel to stop them drying out.

Place one dough portion in a bowl and flatten it slightly. Add the matcha powder, fold the dough over and knead until well blended. Take another dough portion, add a tiny drop of red food colouring, fold the dough over and knead until the dough is a shade of pink.

Roll the white dough into a long log, then cut into eight equal pieces. Roll each piece into a ball about the size of a marble. Repeat with the green and pink doughs.

Bring a large saucepan of water to the boil over medium heat. Working in batches, carefully drop the dumpling balls in the hot water, stirring to stop them sticking to the bottom of the pan. Cook for 3–4 minutes, until they start to float to the surface. Remove with a wire strainer and transfer to a bowl of iced cold water until completely cold.

Drain the dumplings and thread one dumpling of each colour onto a 15 cm (6 in) bamboo skewer – pink on top, white in the middle, and green on the bottom. Drizzle with honey if you desire and enjoy straight away.

JIANSHUI ZONGZI

Be warned, these glutinous rice dumplings are seriously addictive. Much like Hokkien bak chang (page 116), Jianshui zongzi – often called alkaline dumplings – are a festive treat enjoyed during the Dragon Boat (Duanwu) Festival in China, particularly in the Jiangnan region where they originated. Soaking the sticky rice in alkaline water makes the dumpling extra tender and gooey, and imparts a deep yellow colour that's revealed when you unwrap the bamboo leaf.

MAKES 7

500 g (2 cups) glutinous rice

1 tbsp lye water (alkaline water), plus an extra 1 tsp (see note)

1 tbsp vegetable oil, plus extra for brushing

15–20 dried bamboo leaves

150 g (5½ oz) red bean paste (see note, page 149)

white sugar, to serve (optional)

Ingredients continue over page →

Place the glutinous rice in a bowl and pour in enough water to cover the rice by 2.5 cm (1 in). Add the 1 tablespoon of lye water and the vegetable oil and mix well. Cover and soak in the fridge overnight.

The next day, prepare the bamboo leaves. Fully submerge the leaves in water and soak for 1 hour. Drain, place the leaves in a large saucepan, then fill with water until fully submerged. Boil the leaves over high heat for 10 minutes to soften them. Drain, rinse and wipe dry. Trim off the hard stems, brush the oil on the shiny side of the leaves and set aside.

Wash the rice a few times to rinse off the lye water. Drain and set aside in a bowl.

Roll the red bean paste into small balls about the size of a cherry tomato (about 20 g/¾ oz each). Set aside on a plate.

Set up a dumpling wrapping station with the bamboo leaves, the bowl of rice, plate of red bean paste balls, kitchen twine and a pair of scissors.

Take two bamboo leaves and stack them on top of each other. Wrap and fold half the leaves (trimmed end) into a cone shape. Now hold the cone with one hand, add 1 tablespoon of the rice and press lightly to fill the corner at the bottom tip of the cone. Place a red bean paste ball inside, then fill the cone with more rice, pressing down lightly, just enough to cover the red bean paste ball. Fold the short edges of the cone inwards, covering the rice. Now fold the long end of the leaves and wrap around tightly to seal the filling completely. The dumpling should look like a pyramid. Securely wrap the dumpling with kitchen twine and tie it up with double knots. Repeat with the remaining filling and bamboo leaves.

PALM SUGAR SYRUP

300 g (10½ oz) palm sugar, shaved

250 ml (1 cup) water

2 fresh or frozen (thawed) pandan leaves, tied into a knot

Arrange all the dumplings neatly and snugly in a large saucepan. Pour in enough water to cover the top of the dumplings by about 2.5 cm (1 in). Add the remaining 1 teaspoon of lye water, then place a heatproof plate on top of the dumplings to keep them submerged during cooking. Bring the water to the boil over medium–high heat. Once boiling, reduce the heat to medium–low, then cover and simmer for 3 hours. Check the water level periodically, replenishing with boiling water to keep the dumplings fully submerged. Once cooked, remove the dumplings and leave to cool to room temperature.

Place all the palm sugar syrup ingredients in a small saucepan and bring to the boil over medium–high heat. Stir until the sugar has dissolved. Reduce the heat to medium–low, stirring occasionally, and simmer for 5 minutes, or until the mixture has thickened. Remove the pandan leaves and set aside to cool completely.

Serve the dumplings with the palm sugar syrup, or simply dip them in white sugar.

NOTE: You can find lye water at Asian supermarkets. Alkaline water will make the dumplings bouncy, creating a better mouthfeel, and also gives them their distinctive yellow colour. It is also a natural preservative, so the dumplings can be stored longer. They will keep in an airtight container in the fridge for 1 week, or 3 months in the freezer.

DUMPLINGS   Pictured overleaf

1. Jianshui zongzi (page 154)

DUMPLINGS　　2. Nyonya kueh koci (page 158)　　**157**

NYONYA KUEH KOCI

You'll find sweet tooth lovers all across Malaysia, Singapore, Indonesia and Brunei eating kueh koci from breakfast to dessert. A traditional sweet of the Peranakan culture (Chinese people with Malay or Indonesian heritage), these bite-sized rice dumplings fuse popular Malay ingredients (coconut, palm sugar and pandan) with Chinese cooking techniques. Anyone who loves mochi is bound to love kueh koci.

MAKES 10–12

banana leaves (see note), cut into 17 cm (6¾ in) squares; you'll need 10–15 pieces

vegetable oil, for greasing

FILLING

100 g (3½ oz) shredded coconut

60 ml (¼ cup) hot water

80 g (2¾ oz) palm sugar

20 g (¾ oz) dark brown sugar

125 ml (½ cup) coconut milk

2 fresh or frozen (thawed) pandan leaves, tied into a knot

1 tsp cornflour (corn starch), mixed with 1 tbsp water

Ingredients continue over page →

To make the filling, place the shredded coconut and hot water in a heatproof bowl, then stir and set aside for 10 minutes to rehydrate.

Place the palm sugar, brown sugar, coconut milk and pandan leaves in a saucepan and bring to a simmer over medium heat. Stirring occasionally, simmer for about 2 minutes, until the sugar has dissolved. Remove the pandan leaves. Stir in the cornflour slurry, then add the rehydrated coconut. Reduce the heat to low and stir continuously for about 5 minutes, until all the liquid has evaporated. Remove from the heat and leave to cool to room temperature, then roll into balls the size of golf balls (about 15 g/½ oz each).

To make the dough, place the pandan leaves in a blender with 125 ml (½ cup) of the water and blend into a juice. Pour the mixture into a sieve lined with a clean piece of muslin (cheesecloth) over a jug. Squeeze all the juice out, then discard the solids.

Place the glutinous rice flour in a heatproof bowl with the salt and sugar. Mix well and set aside.

Mix the rice flour, vegetable oil and remaining 100 ml (3½ fl oz) of water in a small saucepan. Stir the mixture continuously over medium heat until it turns into a thick paste. Remove from the heat, pour the hot paste over the glutinous rice flour mixture and use chopsticks to mix everything together. Once cool enough to handle, use your hands to rub the flour mixture into crumbs. Add the coconut milk and half the pandan juice and mix until the flour mixture comes together, then add the remaining pandan juice and knead in the bowl into a smooth dough. Cover with a tea towel to stop the dough drying out.

DOUGH

10 fresh or frozen pandan leaves, cut into 3–4 cm (1¼–1½ in) pieces (see note)

225 ml (7½ fl oz) water

200 g (7 oz) glutinous rice flour

pinch of salt

2 tsp caster (superfine) sugar

1 tsp rice flour

1 tbsp vegetable oil

2 tbsp coconut milk

Grease your hands by dipping your fingers in vegetable oil. Tear off a small piece of dough about the size of a golf ball (35 g/1¼ oz) and roll it into a ball. Press your thumb in the centre and shape the dough into a cup. Place a ball of coconut filling in the cup, pinch the dough edges together to seal, then roll it back into a ball. Repeat with the remaining dough and filling.

Prepare the banana leaves by blanching them in hot water for about 30 seconds, until softened. Drain and wipe dry, then grease each leaf with oil.

Fold a banana leaf square into an upside-down cone shape, put a filled dough ball inside and press down lightly to fill the gap at the bottom tip of the cone. Fold the shorter ends inward, then fold the pointy ends from each side inwards to seal and form a flat base for the dumpling to sit on. Use a toothpick to secure the bottom so it doesn't come loose.

Line a large bamboo steamer basket with a round sheet of baking paper with a few holes punched in it (see page 12). Place all the dumplings in the steamer. Cover and steam over a wok of hot simmering water over medium heat for 12 minutes, until cooked. Remove from the heat and leave to cool. Serve at room temperature.

The dumplings will keep in an airtight container in the fridge for up to 3 days, or in the freezer for up to 3 months.

NOTE: You can use either fresh or frozen banana leaves, both of which can be found in Asian supermarkets. Remember to clean the leaves and soften them by blanching them in hot water until softened.

If you can't find pandan leaves, you can use ½ teaspoon pandan essence mixed with 60 ml (¼ cup) water for the dough recipe.

Pictured previous

BASIC DUMPLING WRAPPERS

MAKES 30

250 g (9 oz) plain (all-purpose) flour, plus extra for dusting

pinch of salt

80 ml (⅓ cup) boiling water

60 ml (¼ cup) water, at room temperature

Place the flour and salt in a large bowl and mix well. Pour the boiling water over the flour, stirring with a pair of chopsticks until all the water is absorbed. Stir the room-temperature water through.

Using your hands, knead the flour mixture into a rough dough. Cover and leave to rest for 10–15 minutes, then knead again into a smooth dough. If the dough is still stiff and rough, let it rest for another 10 minutes and knead again.

Finally, rest the dough for a further 30 minutes to 1 hour, until soft.

Transfer the dough to a floured work surface and roll it into a long log about 2.5 cm (1 in) thick. Cut the dough into 30 equal pieces, weighing about 12 g (¼ oz) each, and keep them covered to stop them drying out.

Using the palm of your hand, slightly flatten a piece of dough, then use a rolling pin to roll it out into a thin wrapper, about 10 cm (4 in) in diameter. Repeat with the remaining dough, dusting the wrappers lightly with flour before stacking, to stop them sticking together.

Use the wrappers immediately.

CRYSTAL DUMPLING WRAPPERS

MAKES ABOUT 30

150 g (5½ oz) wheat starch

100 g (3½ oz) potato starch

250 ml (1 cup) boiling water

15 g (½ oz) pork lard

Place the wheat starch and 50 g (1¾ oz) of the potato starch in a large bowl and stir to combine. Carefully pour in the boiling water and stir until all the water has been absorbed. Let the mixture rest for 1 minute, then stir again to form a very sticky mess.

Once cool enough to handle, add the remaining potato starch and knead by hand for 2–3 minutes, until smooth. Add the lard and continue to knead for another minute to form a smooth elastic dough.

Tip the dough onto your work surface (it doesn't need to be floured). Cut the dough into small pieces, weighing about 15 g (½ oz) each, and keep them in a container to stop them drying out. (The dough can sit in the covered container at room temperature for 3 hours at most.)

Using the palm of your hand, slightly flatten a piece of dough, then use a rolling pin and roll it out into a thin wrapper, about 10–11 cm (4–4¼ in) in diameter.

Fill the wrapper with the filling of your choice and fold into a dumpling before rolling out another piece of dough.

WONTON WRAPPERS

MAKES 30

300 g (10½ oz) plain (all-purpose) flour, plus extra for dusting

pinch of salt

1 egg

90 ml (3 fl oz) water, at room temperature

Place the flour, salt and egg in a large bowl and mix well. Stir in the water a little bit at a time until fully incorporated. Using your hands, knead the dough together to form a rough dough. Cover and leave to rest for 30 minutes. Knead the dough again for 3 minutes, until smooth, then rest the dough for a final 30 minutes.

Use a pasta rolling machine, and working from the thickest to the thinnest setting, roll the dough through the machine a few times, into a long thin sheet about 1–2 mm (1/16 in) thick.

With the help of a ruler, cut the dough into 8 cm (3¼ in) squares. Be sure to dust the wrappers lightly with flour before stacking, to stop them sticking together, and use within 2 hours.

XIAO LONG BAO DOUGH

MAKES 18 PIECES

100 g (3½ oz) 00 flour (high-gluten flour)

100 g (3½ oz) plain (all-purpose) flour

2 tsp vegetable oil

½ tsp salt

140 ml (4½ fl oz) boiling water

Place the flours, vegetable oil and salt in a large bowl and mix well. Pour the boiling water over the flour, stirring with a pair of chopsticks until all the water is absorbed.

Once cool enough to handle, knead the flour mixture into a rough dough. Cover and leave to rest for 30 minutes, then knead again into a smooth dough. If the dough is still stiff and rough, let it rest for another 30 minutes and knead again.

Finally, rest the dough for a further 3 hours, until soft.

Tip the dough onto your work surface (it doesn't need to be floured). Knead the dough, then stretch it into a long log about 2.5 cm (1 in) thick. Cut the dough into 18 equal pieces (see note), weighing about 15 g (½ oz) each, and place them in a container to stop them drying out.

The dough can sit in the covered container at room temperature for a maximum of 6 hours, before it gets too soft to make dumplings. Roll them out, one piece at a time, following the Xiao long bao folding technique on page 175, or as directed in your recipe.

NOTE: If using the dough for the crab tang bao dumplings on page 26, cut the dough into four large 45 g (1½ oz) portions.

GLUTEN-FREE DUMPLING WRAPPERS

MAKES 10–12

80 ml (⅓ cup) water, at room temperature, plus an extra 2 tsp

50 g (1¾ oz) tapioca starch

pinch of salt

70 g (2½ oz) rice flour, plus extra for dusting

2 tsp vegetable oil

Combine the water and tapioca starch in a saucepan, stirring to make a smooth, lump-free slurry. Place the pan over low heat and stir constantly. As soon as the mixture starts to thicken, turn off the heat and keep stirring until you have a sticky paste.

Add the salt and 50 g (1¾ oz) of the rice flour, stirring to form a dry flour mixture. Now stir in an extra 1 teaspoon of water at a time to the mixture, until all the flour crumbs come together into a rough dough.

Tip the dough onto a surface lightly dusted with rice flour, then knead until smooth and slightly sticky. Place the remaining 20 g (¾ oz) rice flour on your work surface and smear some of the flour onto the dough as you continue kneading until all the flour is fully incorporated. Add the vegetable oil and knead until combined. The dough should now be smooth, elastic and non-sticky.

Roll the dough into a long log about 2.5 cm (1 in) thick. Cut into small equal pieces, weighing about 14 g (½ oz) each, and place them in a container to stop them drying out.

Using the palm of your hand, slightly flatten a piece of dough, then use a rolling pin to roll it out into a thin wrapper, about 9 cm (3½ in) in diameter.

The wrappers are best used straight away. If you really have to make them in advance, dust them with extra flour, stack them, wrap tightly in plastic wrap and keep in the fridge in a zip-lock bag. They are best used within a few hours, before the condensation gets to them and they start sticking together.

NOTE: You can use these gluten-free wrappers in any recipes that call for the Basic dumpling wrappers (see page 162). However, they aren't suitable as a substitute for other dough recipes.

SOY, VINEGAR & GINGER DIPPING SAUCE

MAKES 200 ML (7 FL OZ)

5 cm (2 in) piece of ginger

80 ml (⅓ cup) Chinkiang black vinegar

80 ml (⅓ cup) light soy sauce

1 tsp sesame oil

Peel the ginger, then cut into thin strips. Place in a small bowl with the vinegar, soy sauce and sesame oil and stir to mix well. This sauce is best used straight away.

CRISPY GARLIC CHILLI OIL

MAKES ABOUT 300 G (10½ OZ)

50 g (1¾ oz) chilli flakes

1 tbsp smoked paprika

1 tbsp soy sauce

1 tsp caster (superfine) sugar

½ tsp MSG

185 ml (¾ cup) vegetable oil

5 French shallots, finely chopped

10 garlic cloves, finely chopped

1 tsp Sichuan peppercorns, crushed

1 small cinnamon stick

2 star anise

3 bay leaves

In a heatproof bowl, mix together the chilli flakes, paprika, soy sauce, sugar and MSG. Set aside.

Heat the vegetable oil in a small saucepan over medium–low heat. Add the shallot, garlic, peppercorns, cinnamon stick, star anise and bay leaves. Stirring occasionally, slowly fry for 20–30 minutes, until the garlic and shallot are crispy and golden brown.

Remove from the heat and leave to cool slightly. Through a fine sieve, carefully pour the infused oil over the chilli mixture. Pick the cinnamon stick, star anise and bay leaves out of the sieve and discard.

Add the remaining crispy bits to the spice and chilli mixture, stirring well. Let the oil infuse overnight before using.

NOTE: The oil will keep in a sealed jar for a month at room temperature.

SICHUAN RED CHILLI OIL

MAKES 200 G (7 OZ)

CHILLI MIX

40 g (1½ oz) chilli flakes

1 tsp salt

1 tsp white sugar

½ tsp white pepper

1 tbsp vegetable oil

1 tbsp sesame seeds

INFUSED OIL

125 ml (½ cup) vegetable oil

2.5 cm (1 in) piece of ginger, julienned

3 garlic cloves, finely chopped

2 spring onions (scallions), white part, sliced

½ red onion, finely sliced

1 bunch coriander (cilantro), chopped

2 bay leaves

1 star anise

2 tsp Sichuan peppercorns

1 small cinnamon stick

To prepare the chilli mix, place the chilli flakes, salt, sugar and white pepper in a heatproof bowl and mix well. Add the vegetable oil and stir until fully absorbed by the chilli. Add the sesame seeds, give the mixture a quick stir and set aside.

To prepare the infused oil, heat the oil in a small saucepan over medium–high heat. Test the oil by dipping a wooden chopstick in the hot oil; it is ready when oil bubbles around the chopstick. Add the ginger, garlic and spring onion and give the oil a stir. Add the onion and coriander, reduce the heat to medium–low and keep stirring for 2–3 minutes to infuse the oil. Add the bay leaves, star anise, peppercorns and cinnamon stick and fry for another 2–3 minutes, until fragrant. Using a wire strainer, scoop out and discard the solids.

Carefully, one ladleful at a time, pour the hot fragrant oil over the chilli flakes, then stir to mix well. Let the oil infuse overnight before using.

NOTE: The oil will keep in a sealed jar for a month at room temperature.

NUOC CHAM

MAKES 300 ML (10 FL OZ)

80 ml (⅓ cup) lime juice (from about 2 limes)

80 ml (⅓ cup) fish sauce

125 ml (½ cup) water

2 tbsp caster (superfine) sugar

2 garlic cloves, minced

2 bird's eye chillies, finely chopped

Place the lime juice, fish sauce, water and sugar in a jug and stir until the sugar has dissolved. Add the garlic and chilli and mix well.

Set aside for at least 1 hour to let the flavours develop before using.

NOTE: The nuoc cham will keep for a month in a sealed jar in the fridge.

DIM SUM CHILLI SAUCE

MAKES ABOUT 180 ML (6 FL OZ)

8 long red chillies, deseeded and roughly chopped

20 g (¾ oz) ginger, finely sliced

8–10 garlic cloves, peeled

2 tbsp calamansi lime juice (see note)

80 ml (⅓ cup) water

50 g (1¾ oz) caster (superfine) sugar

1½ tsp salt

Place the chillies, ginger, garlic, lime juice and water in a blender and blitz into a puree.

Pour the puree into a saucepan, add the sugar and salt and stir to combine. Warm the mixture over medium–high heat until it starts to bubble, then reduce the heat to low and simmer for 15 minutes, stirring occasionally. Remove from the heat and leave to cool completely.

The oil will keep in a sealed jar for a month at room temperature.

NOTE: Calamansi lime is also known as a calamansi cumquat and is sold in many Asian supermarkets (especially Thai and Filipino ones). Alternatively, you can use the juice of regular limes here.

THAI SWEET CHILLI SAUCE

MAKES ABOUT 270 ML (9 FL OZ)

4 long red chillies, stems removed

2 bird's eye chillies, stems removed

3–4 garlic cloves, peeled

150 ml (5 fl oz) water

100 g (3½ oz) caster (superfine) sugar

2 tbsp white vinegar

1 tbsp fish sauce

½ tsp salt

1 tbsp cornflour (corn starch), mixed with 2 tbsp water

Place all the chillies and garlic in a food processor and pulse until finely chopped.

Transfer the chilli mixture to a small saucepan. Add the water, sugar, vinegar, fish sauce and salt and place over medium–high heat. When the mixture starts to boil, reduce the heat to low and simmer for 5 minutes to let the flavours develop.

Give the cornflour slurry a quick stir, pour it into the mixture and stir until it thickens. Simmer for another minute, remove from the heat and let cool completely.

NOTE: The sauce will keep for a month in a sealed jar in the fridge.

TOMATO ACHAR

MAKES ABOUT 450 ML (15 FL OZ)

2 tbsp vegetable oil

1 tbsp minced garlic

1 tbsp minced ginger

4–5 small green chillies, deseeded and roughly chopped

1 red onion, diced

3 large tomatoes, roughly chopped

1 tsp salt

½ tsp ground turmeric

1 tsp ground cumin

1 tsp ground coriander

½ tsp chilli powder

50 g (⅓ cup) sesame seeds, toasted

125 ml (½ cup) water

3 tbsp roughly chopped coriander (cilantro) leaves

Heat the vegetable oil in a frying pan over medium–high heat. Add the garlic, ginger and chilli and stir-fry for about a minute, until fragrant. Add the onion and saute for another minute, or until lightly browned. Stir in the tomatoes, mixing well. Cover the pan with a lid and steam for 2 minutes.

Stir in the salt, ground spices and chilli powder until combined. Cover the pan and reduce the heat to medium. Stirring occasionally, cook for 2 minutes, until the tomatoes have softened. Remove from the heat and set aside to cool.

Place the sesame seeds in a blender and blitz into a powder. Add the cooked tomato mixture and the water and blitz into a smooth puree. Add the coriander leaves and blitz again until smooth.

NOTE: The sauce will keep for a week in a sealed jar in the fridge.

PICKLED GREEN CHILLIES WITH SOY SAUCE

MAKES ABOUT 375 ML (1½ CUPS)

250 ml (1 cup) white vinegar

125 ml (½ cup) water

2 tbsp caster (superfine) sugar

10–12 green chillies, finely sliced

2 tsp salt

light soy sauce, to taste

Warm the vinegar, water and sugar in a small saucepan over medium heat, stirring and simmering until the sugar has dissolved. Remove from the heat and cool to room temperature.

Place the chilli slices in a mixing bowl. Sprinkle the salt over, stir to mix well, then transfer to a sterilised heatproof glass jar.

Pour the vinegar mixture over the chilli slices, making sure they are fully submerged. Add more water if needed.

Seal the lid on the jar, then give it a few shakes to mix well. Leave to pickle at room temperature overnight before using; the flavour will develop further with longer pickling.

To serve, place a spoonful of pickled chillies in a saucer and drizzle with soy sauce to taste.

NOTE: The pickles will keep for up to 1 month at room temperature, or up to 3 months in the fridge.

YANGNYEOM JANG

MAKES ABOUT 150 ML (5½ FL OZ)

60 ml (¼ cup) light soy sauce

60 ml (¼ cup) water

1 tbsp rice vinegar

1 tbsp caster (superfine) sugar

1 tbsp gochugaru (Korean chilli flakes)

1 tbsp sesame seeds, lightly toasted

2 garlic cloves, minced

2 spring onions (scallions), finely sliced

1 red bird's eye chilli, finely chopped

Combine all the ingredients in a large bowl, stirring until the sugar has dissolved.

Cover and leave to sit for at least 2 hours to let the flavours develop.

NOTE: The sauce will keep in a sealed jar in the fridge for up to 1 month.

JELLIED STOCK

MAKES ABOUT 400 G (14 OZ)

250 g (9 oz) piece of pork rind, cut into 1 cm (½ in) strips

2 tsp salt

3 slices ginger

1 spring onion (scallion), cut into 5 cm (2 in) lengths

1 tbsp Shaoxing rice wine

Place the pork rind in a saucepan and pour in 500 ml (2 cups) water. Bring to a rolling boil over high heat. Let the water boil for 2 minutes, then drain the pan. Rinse the pork rind to remove any impurities.

Rinse out the pan, put the pork back in and pour in another 500 ml (2 cups) fresh water. Add the remaining ingredients and bring to the boil over high heat. Reduce the heat to low, then cover and simmer for 2 hours.

Remove from the heat and set aside to cool a little. Carefully pour the liquid through a sieve into a heatproof bowl and leave to cool to room temperature.

Cover and leave in the fridge overnight, where the stock will set into a jelly. It will keep refrigerated for up to 5 days, or can be frozen for longer storage.

VEGETABLE STOCK

MAKES ABOUT 1.5 LITRES (6 CUPS)

2 tbsp vegetable oil

1 large onion, finely diced

2.5 cm (1 in) piece of ginger, finely sliced

2 carrots, diced

2 celery sticks, diced

3–4 spring onions (scallions), cut into 5 cm (2 in) lengths

2–3 star anise

1 tbsp salt

1 tsp black peppercorns

Heat the vegetable oil in a large stockpot over medium–high heat. Add the onion, ginger, carrot and celery and saute for 3–4 minutes, until lightly browned. Pour in 3 litres (12 cups) water, add the remaining ingredients and bring to the boil. Skim off any impurities on the surface with a ladle.

Reduce the heat to low and simmer uncovered for 3 hours, or until the stock has reduced by half.

Strain the stock through a piece of muslin (cheesecloth) into another pot or heatproof container. It is now ready to be used, or will keep in the fridge for up to 5 days.

PHO STOCK

MAKES ABOUT 1.5 LITRES (6 CUPS)

4 large red Asian shallots, halved

10 cm (4 in) piece of ginger, halved lengthways

8 cloves

5 star anise

2 cinnamon sticks

1 tbsp coriander seeds

1 tbsp black peppercorns

2 kg (4 lb 6 oz) beef bones (a mix of knuckles, legs or oxtails)

60 ml (¼ cup) fish sauce

50 g (1¾ oz) rock sugar (see note)

1 tbsp salt

Switch on a gas stove on low flame. Place the shallots and ginger directly on the naked flame, turning frequently with tongs until charred all over. Leave until cool enough to handle, then peel off any blackened bits and set aside. (Alternatively, you can grill the shallots and ginger on a barbecue, or using the overhead grill in your oven.)

Toast the cloves, star anise, cinnamon sticks, coriander seeds and peppercorns in a frying pan over medium heat for 3 minutes, or until fragrant. Leave to cool, then place the spices in a muslin (cheesecloth) pouch and tie with kitchen twine.

Place the bones in a large stockpot and fill with enough water to fully submerge all the bones. Bring to a rolling boil over high heat, then leave to boil for 5 minutes. Drain the pan, rinse the bones and clean the pan. Return the bones to the pan and fill with 3 litres (12 cups) fresh water.

Add the spice pouch and the charred shallots and ginger. Bring to the boil over high heat. Skim off any impurities on the surface with a ladle. Reduce the heat to low. Add the fish sauce, rock sugar and salt, then simmer uncovered for 3 hours, or until the stock is almost reduced by half. Taste and adjust the seasoning accordingly.

Strain the stock through a piece of muslin into another pot or heatproof container. It is now ready to be used, or will keep in the fridge for up to 3 days.

NOTE: To make a thicker jellied pho stock for the Pho soup dumplings on page 24, simmer the stock for a further 1 hour or so, until reduced to only 500–810 ml (2–3¼ cups).

FOLD · PINCH

1.

Take a round dumpling wrapper and place a heaped teaspoon of filling in the centre.

2.

Fold the wrapper in half and pinch the centre together using your fingertips.

3.

To seal, press the edge of the dumpling between your thumbs and the edge of your index fingers. Press firmly to seal, gently bringing the dumpling ends inwards to form a plump centre.

4.

Your dumpling is ready to steam, boil or cook in any of the recipes.

FOLD · XIAO LONG BAO

1. Using the palm of your hand, slightly flatten a piece of dough, then use a rolling pin and roll it out into a thin wrapper, about 11 cm (4¼ in) in diameter.

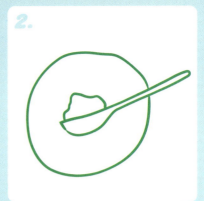

2. Place the wrapper in the palm of your non-dominant hand and scoop a heaped tablespoon of filling (about 20 g/¾ oz) in the centre.

3. Gently pull the edge of the dumpling wrapper with your dominant hand and fold to make a small pleat. Working in a counter-clockwise direction, continue to stretch the dough and make pleats next to each other.

4. Repeat all the way around, leaving a small vent hole in the centre so the dumpling won't 'explode' when steamed.

FOLD • GOLD INGOT

1.

Take a square dumpling wrapper and place a heaped teaspoon of filling in the centre.

2.

Fold the wrapper in half, into a triangle. Press around the filling to remove any air pockets, then pinch the edges together to seal.

3.

Rest the dumpling on a work surface with the folded side of the dumpling closest to you. Bring the two base points of the triangle down until they meet in the middle.

4.

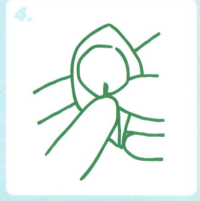

Press the two edges together to seal.

NOTE: You can use this technique with circular wrappers too, for a slightly different look (see XO scallop and prawn dumplings on page 17).

FOLD • GYOZA

1.

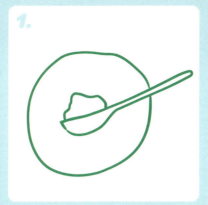

Take a round dumpling wrapper and place a heaped teaspoon of filling in the centre.

2.

Fold the wrapper in half, into a semi-circle. Gently pinch the edges in the centre to help keep the shape.

3.

Starting from one side of the dumpling, fold the front edge of the wrapper towards the centre, then press to form a small pleat.

4.

Repeat along the edge until you reach the end and the dumpling is fully sealed.

DUMPLINGS

FOLD • BAMBOO LEAVES

1.

To prepare the bamboo leaves, fully submerge the dried leaves in water for 1 hour. Drain, place in a large saucepan, fill with water until fully submerged and boil for 10 minutes to soften. Drain, rinse and wipe dry. Trim off the hard stems and brush with vegetable oil on the shiny side of the leaves.

2.

Stack two bamboo leaves over each other, slightly offset, with the oiled sides facing up. Eyeball a point about two-thirds along the width of the bamboo leaves so there is a long side and a short side. Bring the longer side towards you, then under and behind the shorter side.

3.

You should end up with a cone shape that resembles the illustration above. You want the short side of the bamboo leaf on the inside and the longer side on the outside. This will help when filling and bundling the parcel.

4.

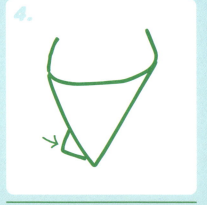

Adjust the tip of the cone to make sure there is some overlap at the pointed tip. This will stop the filling from falling out when you fill the bamboo leaf.

FOLDING TECHNIQUES

5. Hold the cone with one hand, add a layer of rice (or dough, depending on the recipe), and press it down lightly to fill the tip of the cone. Top with the filling, then fill the cone with more rice (or dough), pressing down firmly.

6. Fold the shorter flap of leaves over the filling to secure it, then fold the longer flap over the top.

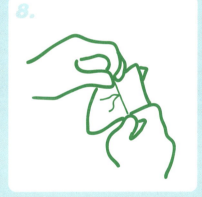

7. Firmly wrap the leaves around to form a pyramid-shaped parcel, sealing the filling completely.

8. Securely wrap the dumpling with kitchen twine and tie a double knot, so the dumpling won't unravel during steaming. Smaller dumplings can be secured with a toothpick (see Nyonya kueh koci on page 158).

INDEX

B

Baiyu jiaozi 101
bamboo leaves
  fold 178–9
  Jianshui zongzi 154–5
  Sago zongzi 146
bamboo shoots, Har gow 14
banana leaves, Nyonya kueh koci 158–9
Banh bot loc 112–13
Banh it tran 48–9
Basic dumpling wrappers 162
bean sprouts, Kimchi & pork mandu 84
beef
  Beef & celery dumplings 110
  Beef dumpling pho soup 126–7
  Pho soup dumplings 24
  Pho stock 173
  Spicy Thai-style beef dumplings 68
Black sesame tang yuan 142–3
Bukkumi 149

C

cabbage
  Pan-fried rice paper veggie dumplings 86
  Traditional Japanese pork gyozas 72
  Vegetable momos 32
  Vegetarian dumpling miso soup 120
carrots
  Chai kueh 44
  Chicken & shiitake dumplings 98
  Pan-fried rice paper veggie dumplings 86
  Prawn crystal flower dumplings 42–3
  Vegan mushroom & cabbage dumplings 92
  Vegetable momos 32
  Vegetable stock 172
  Vegetarian bao 23
  Vegetarian dumpling miso soup 120
celery
  Beef & celery dumplings 110
  Ham sui gok 60–1
  Teochew dumplings 38–9
  Vegetable stock 172
Chai kueh 44
chestnuts
  Hokkien bak chang 116–17
  see also water chestnuts
chicken
  Chicken & corn dumpling soup 130
  Chicken & shiitake dumplings 98
  Chicken & wombok jade dumplings 96
  Chicken wonton laksa soup 133
  Pangsit goreng 71
  Sweet potato & chicken dumplings 47
chilli oil
  Chilli oil dressing 104
  Crispy garlic chilli oil 165
  Sichuan red chilli oil 166
chillies
  Lamb momos 30
  Pickled green chillies with soy sauce 170
  Prawn wonton tom yum soup 134
  Spicy pumpkin & tofu dumplings 95
  Spicy Thai-style beef dumplings 68
  Thai sweet chilli sauce 168
  Tomato achar 169
  Vegetable momos 32
  Yangnyeom jang 171
  Dim sum chilli sauce 167
chives
  Baiyu jiaozi 101
  Ku chai kueh 29
  Prawn & chive dumplings 102
  Prawn gyozas with crispy skirt 74
  Teochew dumplings 38–9
  Water chestnut & leek dumplings 78
cilantro *see* coriander
coconut/coconut milk
  Chicken wonton laksa soup 133
  Coconut syrup 150
  Gok zai 144
  Nyonya kueh koci 158–9
coriander
  Pho soup dumplings 24
  Pork & coriander jiaozi 108
  Saku sai moo 52–3
  Sichuan lamb dumplings 80
  Teochew dumplings 38–9
  Vegan mushroom & cabbage dumplings 92
  Vegetable momos 32
  Vegetarian dumpling miso soup 120
  XO scallop & prawn dumplings 17
corn
  Chicken & corn dumpling soup 130
  Chicken & shiitake dumplings 98
courgettes *see* zucchini
crab
  Crab & pork xiao long bao 20
  Crab tang bao 26
  Hai choe 64–5

Crispy garlic chilli oil 165
Crystal dumpling wrappers 162
Crystal jade wrappers 118
cucumber, Peking duck dumplings 83

dipping sauces 71, 112–13
  Nuoc cham 167
  Soy, vinegar & ginger dipping sauce 165
dried shrimp *see* shrimp, dried
duck, Peking duck dumplings 83

eggs, Zucchini & egg jiaozi 90

fish, Baiyu jiaozi 101
folds
  bamboo leaves 178–9
  gold ingot 176
  gyoza 177
  pinch 174
  xiao long bao 174
Fried prawn wontons 56

garlic chives *see* chives
ginger
  Ginger & spring onion water 18, 24, 101, 107, 110, 126–7
  Ginger brown sugar syrup 139
  Pho stock 173
Gluten-free dumpling wrappers 164
glutinous rice/glutinous rice flour
  Glutinous rice dough 49, 60–1, 138, 142, 149

Hanami dango 152
Hokkien bak chang 116–17
Jianshui zongzi 154–5
Gok zai 144
Gold ingot fold 176
gyozas
  fold 177
  Prawn gyozas with crispy skirt 74
  Traditional Japanese pork gyozas 72

Hai choe 64–5
Hakka crystal jade pork & leek dumplings 118
Ham sui gok 60–1
Hanami dango 152
Har gow 14
Hobak mandu 36
Hokkien bak chang 116–17

Jellied stock 172
Jianshui zongzi 154–5
jiaozi
  Baiyu jiaozi 101
  Pork & coriander jiaozi 108
  Pork & prawn jiaozi 107
  Zucchini & egg jiaozi 90
jicama
  Chai kueh 44
  Teochew dumplings 38–9

Kimchi & pork mandu 84
Krong krang nam kati 150
Ku chai kueh 29

laksa, Chicken wonton laksa soup 133

lamb
  Lamb momos 30
  Sichuan lamb dumplings 80
leeks
  Hakka crystal jade pork & leek dumplings 118
  Water chestnut & leek dumplings 78
lime juice
  Nuoc cham 167
  Dim sum chilli sauce 167
lime leaves, Prawn wonton tom yum soup 134

mandu
  Hobak mandu 36
  Kimchi & pork mandu 84
  Pork mandu 35
Marinades 12, 30, 83
Miso soup 120
mung beans, Banh it tran 48–9
mushrooms
  Chicken & shiitake dumplings 98
  Chicken & wombok jade dumplings 96
  Ham sui gok 60–1
  Hobak mandu 36
  Hokkien bak chang 116–17
  Mushroom & water chestnut wonton soup 123
  Pan-fried rice paper veggie dumplings 86
  Prawn wonton tom yum soup 134
  Siu mai 12
  Spicy pumpkin & tofu dumplings 95
  Teochew dumplings 38–9
  Tofu & mushroom potstickers 77

DUMPLINGS *181*

Vegan mushroom & cabbage dumplings 92
Vegetarian bao 12, 23
Vegetarian dumpling miso soup 120

noodles
　Kimchi & pork mandu 84
　Pork mandu 35
　Vegan mushroom & cabbage dumplings 92
Nuoc cham 167
Nyonya kueh koci 158–9

onions, Vegetable stock 172

Palm sugar syrup 154–5
Pan-fried pork wontons 58
Pan-fried rice paper veggie dumplings 86
pandan leaves
　Ginger brown sugar syrup 139
　Nyonya kueh koci 158–9
　Palm sugar syrup 154–5
　Sweet soy milk 143
Pangsit goreng 71
peanuts
　Gok zai 144
　Peanut tang yuan 138–9
　Saku sai moo 52–3
　Teochew dumplings 38–9
Peking duck dumplings 83
pho
　Beef dumpling pho soup 126–7
　Pho soup dumplings 24
　Pho stock 173
Pickled green chillies with soy sauce 170
Pinch fold 174
Pink wrapper dough 43
pork
　Banh bot loc 112–13
　Banh it tran 48–9
　Crab & pork xiao long bao 20

Hai choe 64–5
Hakka crystal jade pork & leek dumplings 118
Ham sui gok 60–1
Hokkien bak chang 116–17
Jellied stock 172
Kimchi & pork mandu 84
Pan-fried pork wontons 58
Pork & coriander jiaozi 108
Pork & prawn jiaozi 107
Pork & prawn wonton soup 124
Pork mandu 35
Pork xiao long bao 18
Red chilli oil pork dumplings 104
Saku sai moo 52–3
Siu mai 12
Teochew dumplings 38–9
Thung thong 66
Traditional Japanese pork gyozas 72
prawns
　Banh bot loc 112–13
　Banh it tran 48–9
　Fried prawn wontons 56
　Hai choe 64–5
　Har gow 14
　Pork & prawn jiaozi 107
　Pork & prawn wonton soup 124
　Prawn & chive dumplings 102
　Prawn crystal flower dumplings 42–3
　Prawn gyozas with crispy skirt 74
　Prawn wonton tom yum soup 134
　Siu mai 12
　Thung thong 66
　XO scallop & prawn dumplings 17
pumpkin, Spicy pumpkin & tofu dumplings 95

radish, preserved
　Saku sai moo 52–3
　Teochew dumplings 38–9

red bean paste
　Bukkumi 149
　Jianshui zongzi 154–5
　Sago zongzi 146
Red chilli oil pork dumplings 104

Sago zongzi 146
Saku sai moo 52–3
sauces
　Thai sweet chilli sauce 168
　Tomato achar 169
　Yangnyeom jang 171
　Dim sum chilli sauce 167
　see also dipping sauces
scallops, XO scallop & prawn dumplings 17
sesame seeds
　Black sesame tang yuan 142–3
　Gok zai 144
　Tomato achar 169
shallots
　Pho stock 173
　Shallot oil 116
shrimp, dried
　Banh it tran 48–9
　Chai kueh 44
　Ham sui gok 60–1
　Hokkien bak chang 116–17
　Ku chai kueh 29
　Teochew dumplings 38–9
　Zucchini & egg jiaozi 90
Sichuan lamb dumplings 80
Sichuan red chilli oil 166
Siu mai 12
soups
　Beef dumpling pho soup 126–7
　Chicken & corn dumpling soup 130
　Chicken wonton laksa soup 133
　Mushroom & water chestnut wonton soup 123
　Pork & prawn wonton soup 124
　Prawn wonton tom yum soup 134
　Vegetarian dumpling miso soup 120

Soy, vinegar & ginger dipping sauce 165
Spicy pumpkin & tofu dumplings 95
Spicy Thai-style beef dumplings 68
Spinach dough 96
spring onions
 Ginger & spring onion water 18, 24, 101, 107, 110, 126–7
 Pork & coriander jiaozi 108
 Spring onion oil 112–13
 Thung thong 66
 Vegetable stock 172
stock
 Jellied stock 172
 Pho stock 173
 Vegetable stock 172
sweet potato
 Sweet potato & chicken dumplings 47
 Sweet potato dough 47
Sweet soy milk 143

tang yuan
 Black sesame tang yuan 142–3
 Peanut tang yan 138–9
Tapioca dough 113
tapioca flour, Krong krang nam kati 150
tapioca pearls
 Sago zongzi 146
 Saku sai moo 52–3
Teochew dumplings 38–9
Thai sweet chilli sauce 168
Thung thong 66
tofu
 Hobak mandu 36
 Kimchi & pork mandu 84
 Pan-fried rice paper veggie dumplings 86
 Spicy pumpkin & tofu dumplings 95
 Tofu & mushroom potstickers 77
 Vegan mushroom & cabbage dumplings 92

Vegetable momos 32
Vegetarian bao 23
Vegetarian dumpling miso soup 120
tom yum, Prawn wonton tom yum soup 134
Tomato achar 169
Traditional Japanese pork gyozas 72

vegan
 Pan-fried rice paper veggie dumplings 86
 Vegan mushroom & cabbage dumplings 92
Vegetable momos 32
Vegetable stock 172
vegetarian
 Hobak mandu 36
 Mushroom & water chestnut wonton soup 123
 Spicy pumpkin & tofu dumplings 95
 Tofu & mushroom potstickers 77
 Vegetable momos 32
 Vegetarian bao 23
 Vegetarian dumpling miso soup 120
 Water chestnut & leek dumplings 78
 Zucchini & egg jiaozi 90

walnuts, Black sesame tang yuan 142–3
water chestnuts
 Hai choe 64–5
 Mushroom & water chestnut wonton soup 123
 Prawn gyozas with crispy skirt 74
 Thung thong 66
 Water chestnut & leek dumplings 78
 XO scallop & prawn dumplings 17

White dough 96
wombok
 Chicken & corn dumpling soup 130
 Chicken & wombok jade dumplings 96
 Chicken wonton laksa soup 133
 Pork mandu 35
 Vegetarian bao 23
wontons
 Chicken wonton laksa soup 133
 Fried prawn wontons 56
 Mushroom & water chestnut wonton soup 123
 Pan-fried pork wontons 58
 Pork & prawn wonton soup 124
 Prawn wonton tom yum soup 134
 Wonton wrappers 163
wrappers
 Basic dumpling wrappers 162
 Crystal dumpling wrappers 162
 Crystal jade wrappers 118
 Gluten-free dumpling wrappers 164
 Pink wrapper dough 43
 Wonton wrappers 163

xiao long bao
 Crab & pork xiao long bao 20
 Crab tang bao 26
 fold 175
 Pork xiao ling bao 18
 Xiao long bao dough 163
 XO scallop & prawn dumplings 17

Yangnyeom jang 171
Dim sum chilli sauce 167

zucchini
 Hobak mandu 36
 Zucchini & egg jiaozi 90

DUMPLINGS 183

Published in 2025 by Smith Street Books
Naarm (Melbourne) | Australia
smithstreetbooks.com

Distributed outside of ANZ, North & Latin America by
Thames & Hudson Ltd., 6–24 Britannia Street, London, WC1X 9JD
thamesandhudson.com

EU Authorized Representative: Interart S.A.R.L.
19 rue Charles Auray, 93500 Pantin, Paris, France
productsafety@thameshudson.co.uk; www.interart.fr

ISBN: 978-1-9232-3905-0

All rights reserved. No part of this book may be reproduced or transmitted by any person or entity, in any form or by any means, electronic or mechanical, including photocopying, recording, scanning or by any storage and retrieval system, without the prior written permission of the publishers and copyright holders.

Copyright recipes, text & design © Smith Street Books
Copyright photography © Emily Weaving

Publisher: Paul McNally
Project editor: Elena Callcott
Recipe developer: Billy Law
Editor: Katri Hilden
Design concept & Illustrations: George Saad
Design layout: Nikola Roberts
Introductory text: Melissa Woodley, Elena Callcott
Photographer: Emily Weaving
Stylist: Bridget Wald
Food preparation: Caroline Griffiths
Proofreader: Pamela Dunne
Indexer: Max McMaster
Pre-press: Megan Ellis
Production manager: Aisling Coughlan

Printed & bound in China by C&C Offset Printing Co., Ltd.

Book 397
10 9 8 7 6 5 4 3 2 1